Sermons of Consequence

F. Dean Lueking and
Bruce K. Modahl

Lutheran University Press
Minneapolis, Minnesota

Sermons of Consequence
by F. Dean Lueking and Bruce K. Modahl

Copyright © 2016 F. Dean Lueking. All rights reserved. Published by Lutheran University Press, an imprint of 1517 Media. Except for brief quotations in critical articles or reviews, no part of this book may be reproduced in any manner without prior written permission from the publisher.

ISBN: 978-1-942304-22-7
eISBN: 978-1-942304-77-7

Cover and interior design by Kathryn Hillert Brewer.

Contents

By Way of Introduction 5

SERMONS OF F. DEAN LUEKING

Thy Will Be Done 9
Who Will Follow? 15
The Testimony of the Heart 19
In Newness of Life 23
Ready to Lead 29
A Gift from God 35
Our Debt to Israel 40
What Manner of Spirit Are We? 44
How Far Will God Go? 50
The Call Is Severe, the Caller Merciful 57
Impoverished by Wealth 63
Justice, Kindness, Humility 68
Partners in the Gospel 74
Finding a Lost Reverence for God 80
Mark, the Young Man Who Fled 85

SERMONS OF BRUCE K. MODAHL

Getting Bent into Shape 95
A Time to Mourn 99
The Sentinel's Cry 104
Keep Us from Presumptuous Sins 109
What Then Shall We Say to This? 114
Committed to Mission 118
Responding to the Promise 123
Conspiracy Theory 128
One Little Word 131
A Step Too Far 136

By Way of Introduction

Sermons have consequences.

Some are welcome, surprising both preacher and hearer alike as God's good news reaches its resting point deep in the human heart and brings responses beyond what was desired or deserved.

And sometimes sermons evoke pushback that is hard to take, not at all what the one preaching anticipated when delivering the judgment and grace of God to people well loved. All preachers and those who hear preaching in congregations everywhere know these things.

This book grew out of a sermon on a Romans 10 text that became consequential in a congregation-denomination conflict that went all the way to the Supreme Court before being resolved in our favor. Later on, at the suggestion of church musician Carl Schalk, I broadened the content of the book to include more sermons that were consequential for the wider life of a congregation. Thus it has turned into a unique way of writing a mini history of a congregation based on sermons that were instrumental in telling not only what happened but why events unfolded as they did.

This book is meant for all preachers and laity in congregations of whatever denomination, size, and situation. It is drawn from sermons preached over the past half century at Grace Lutheran Church in the Chicago suburb of River Forest, Illinois. Although the places and people named have local familiarity, the sermons and consequences set forth here speak to the wider human condition with all its varieties that make the book applicable to people everywhere.

Tracing out the signs of the abiding wonder whereby hearers become doers of the Word is all the more needed now. The current mantra "I'm spiritual but don't need the church" is painfully widespread. The underlying premise of this book is that belonging to Christ is inseparable from belonging to people. Preaching and hearing the Good News of God's grace in the gathered congregation is not a drag but a gift, not what we've got to do but what we get to do.

I have selected fifteen sermons representative of my pastoral years at Grace from 1954 to 1998. These appear first in the book, followed by ten sermons graciously contributed by Bruce K. Modahl, Grace's senior pastor from 1998 to 2014. He and I have introduced each of our sermons with a brief comment on its context and consequences.

This needs saying. Many sermon consequences are known only to God and the persons involved. They remain hidden in that sacred space forever beyond human view. Other sermons, however, are marked by wonderfully recognizable signs of God's grace at work. In the interest of full candor this also needs saying: all who preach and all who hear know that some sermons are more forgettable than consequential. Worse yet, some sermons wound deeply, instill prejudice, and stir up violent hatred.

Such things keep us who preach humble, steady in our calling as faithful messengers, and eager to ascribe to God alone the power and glory that is finally and fully consequential.

F. Dean Lueking, Pastor Emeritus,
Grace Lutheran Church,
River Forest, Illinois

Sermons
By *F. Dean Lueking*

Thy Will Be Done
Funeral for Dr. O. A. Geiseman

November 10, 1962
Matthew 6:10
F. Dean Lueking, Preacher

Thy will be done on earth as it is in heaven.
(Matthew 6:10)

Otto A. Geiseman, the fourth pastor of Grace Lutheran Church, served from 1922 until his death in 1962.

His forty-year pastorate established what I think of as "the Grace tradition," meaning a conscious effort to infuse the redeeming love of God in Jesus Christ throughout all aspects of congregational life. It showed specifically in striving for standards of excellence in preaching and worship, encouraging lay leadership, maintaining the congregation and school as one ministry, and moving from its origins as a primarily German Lutheran congregation and school to an openness to all in the community.

During Geiseman's four decades as pastor, the membership increased from 400 to 1500. In the late 1920s Geiseman led the congregation in a bold move from the original church location at Augusta and Belleforte in Oak Park to the Bonnie Brae and Division corner in River Forest. The new and vastly enlarged sanctuary and school was dedicated in 1931, despite the onset of the Great Depression that lasted throughout the 1930s. It was paid for by 1946. Pastor Geiseman's leadership of a devoted congregation throughout that era was summarized by his oft repeated phrase, "whatever you do for the Lord, do your best."

He pioneered ministerial practices uncommon for his or any time, including extensive pastoral counseling to those troubled by daily life conflicts, earning a doctoral degree at a nearby Lutheran seminary while carrying the full load of daily care of the congregation, mentoring a series of newly ordained assistant pastors in the pastoral calling while encouraging them to pursue further graduate study, and participating in community life by joining a local service organization.

His first love was for the people of Grace, a love warmly returned to him by parishioners who could count on him for his guidance in times glad and sad.

While he chafed against and openly criticized his denomination whenever its self-preoccupation threatened the free course of the Gospel, he was nevertheless sought after as a respected pastoral leader in the Lutheran Church–Missouri Synod. He served on its Board of Directors, as well as the governing boards of Valparaiso University, the Lutheran Foundation, the Family Life Committee of the Synod, and Walther Lutheran Hospital in Chicago. He lectured frequently at pastoral conferences, summer camps, and marriage institutes.

His nine published books included volumes of his sermons as well as books on marriage and pastoral ministry. His weekly sermons reached 350 subscribers. From 1936 until 1962 he wrote a monthly column, "While It Is Day," in the American Lutheran magazine, which carried his pastoral wisdom and insights to readers throughout the United States.

His death at 69 on November 7, 1962, ended a remarkably productive ministry. Regrettably, his sermons reflecting particular turning points at Grace, are not available. This summary of highlights of the Geiseman era points to what the Holy Spirit accomplished through the preaching and hearing of the Word at Grace Church from 1922 until 1962. It also reflects what I saw and learned as Pastor Geiseman's assistant and associate from 1954 until 1962, his last eight years at Grace which were also the first eight of my forty-four years at Grace.

The following is the sermon I preached at his funeral on November 10, 1962.

Our hearts are heavy as we come together today. It seems more surreal than real that Pastor Otto Geiseman is not with us. The shock of his death after a long illness hits hard. Each one of us, and many more across the land, have known and loved him as a gifted pastor, preacher, counselor, teacher, churchman, author, and trusted friend. What words can we find that come anywhere close to what we feel now?

Not surprisingly, and consistent with his forty years of pastoral care, he had a scriptural text in mind for us as he thought of this service. A few days ago, knowing that his death was near, he asked me to preach his funeral sermon based on Jesus' words, "Thy will be done on earth as it is in heaven" (Matthew 6:10). He was thinking of us. Though his voice was weak his mind was clear as he said to "point the people to Christ, not to me, and assure them that nothing can separate us from his love."

Let's honor Pastor Geiseman's final wish. We're here to commend him to God and take comfort from that same peace of Christ in which he rests. Let's pray "Thy will be done" with gratitude for his forty years of faithful ministry among us. Let thanksgiving rise up to God and lift us beyond tears and loss. God buries his workmen but his work goes on.

Jesus taught us this petition of the Lord's Prayer in his Sermon on the Mount recorded in the Gospel of St. Matthew. He did more than teach it with words. He prayed it in all earnestness in Gethsemane's Garden on the night of his betrayal. With the full powers of hell pressing in on him he prayed, "Father, if it be thy will, let this cup pass from me." He knew the dread of the death that lay before him, a death beyond our imagining because it bore the weight of the world's sin. In his human nature Jesus prayed for deliverance from suffering. He also went on to pray, "Nevertheless, not my will but thine be done." In his divine nature God's beloved Son was obedient unto death, even death on a cross. And on the third day he rose again to be our living Savior to whom we turn as we bury our pastor and take courage for the future.

By offering up his life upon the cross for us, Jesus broke the bondage of sin and freed us to stand fully known, fully accepted before God. Catch the promise of those words—*for us*! Those two words connect us by faith to the good news of God's grace for the bad news of our sin. God's word is alive and at work among us. We were baptized into it. We now depend upon the Holy Spirit to continually be there for us as we face a new time without a familiar voice and a trusted hand to guide us.

Pastor Geiseman's choice of "Thy will be done" as God's timely word to us now comes as no surprise. It was his own prayer, especially throughout this past year of his daily struggle against cancer. He really wanted to live. He had so much yet to live for with his wife and family and with this congregation that he loved with all his heart. His "Thy will be done" witnesses to the victory of his faith over the death that took him from us at age 69. That prayer glorifies God as the One with the last word over our lives, a saving word that promises a grace and mercy beyond all we could desire or deserve.

Pastor Geiseman's submission to "Thy will be done" is the Spirit's crowning work and confirming seal upon all his preaching, teaching, caring, and counseling throughout his pastoral years. He knew what was in human hearts, the best and the worst, because he knew what was in his own. No wonder, then, his parting wish for us was so clear and strong: "Point people to Christ!"

His ministry indeed touched each of us personally. It is inspiring to see why. Here are turning point moments in his own life when he learned firsthand what "Thy will be done" can lead to.

As a young teenager he enrolled at Concordia High School and College in Milwaukee to begin his education for the pastoral ministry. His initial enthusiasm, however, was dampened by a doctrinaire legalism and loveless orthodoxy he experienced there. From early on he had an instinctive resistance to a Lutheranism more Law than Gospel. He was so discouraged by it that by his senior year he had given up on a pastoral future and was searching for something else. Then, at a school outing just prior to graduation, his friend and classmate drowned. The accident stunned him. He spoke of lying awake all night in a Milwaukee park, wrestling with whether to quit or continue preparation for the ministry. What brought him back to the conviction that he should continue was a chastened awareness that being alive and not dead was meant for some purpose under God. So he kept praying, "Thy will be done," with a deeper awareness that God's will was not to avoid the church's failings but to stay put and do all he could to keep the Gospel front and center as the power for the church to grow more Christ-like.

In his first two pastorates in downstate Illinois he loved the people and the work. Once again, however, he felt the shock of the unexpected. His wife, whom he had met and married in his second pastorate in Pekin, Illinois, died in childbirth, leaving him with a newborn daughter to care for in addition to his daily duties. "Thy will be done" was again the prayer prayed through a hard time and once again faithfully answered. He met and married Marie, his second wife and mother of the children of the Geiseman family. She has been his loving, loyal partner in all the years since. Today we express our sympathies to you, Marie, and to the whole Geiseman family.

Grace congregation was a troubled flock when the Geisemans arrived in Oak Park in 1922. As the story goes, it was a town-gown split that divided some laity from Concordia College faculty parishioners. He dealt with the problem directly. Just before a Christmas Eve service he opened a mean-spirited letter addressed to him by an anonymous member. He was taken aback by its malicious content. At the end of the Christmas Eve service he asked the congregation to be seated. He then read the letter in full, adding that if any parishioner could substantiate even a single accusation he would resign then and there. No one did. He sent the congregation home for a cheerful Christmas Eve with their families and went home to enjoy his own. "Thy will be done" began a healing process in a congregation that needed it.

Some of you present today helped form the congregation's visionary plan in the late 1920s to move the church and school from Oak Park to River Forest. You can also remember the disastrous stock market crash of October 1929 that hit just days after those plans were completed. It's impossible for us who were not there to imagine the challenge of carrying that vision through despite the unprecedented economic hardship of the Great Depression. Think of the mood of the 600 Grace members at the building dedication service in March 1931 as a mixture of joy over its completion and anxiety over the huge debt they faced. It took sacrificial giving through the following fifteen years until the mortgage was burned in 1946. Pastor Geiseman often summed it all up in one woman's story. In the mid-1930s she received the SOS call that went out to all members to meet just the *interest* payment due on the building loan. She decided the new winter coat she was saving for could wait and sent her check to the church instead. There were many more like her.

Another witness to Pastor Geiseman's ministry under "Thy will be done" occurred in 1945. He was among the forty-four pastors and professors of the Lutheran Church–Missouri Synod who published a Synod-wide protest against an encroaching legalism and self-preoccupation that obstructed the free course of the Gospel. A fire storm of reaction followed. Pastor Geiseman stood up to it, as did the Grace Church that backed him. Harsh criticism did not deter either the pastor or the congregation from boldness in calling the Missouri Synod to face its flaws and trust the Holy Spirit for guidance in correcting them.

The Grace tradition and Pastor Geiseman's visionary leadership showed again in the late 1940s when he initiated something new in the Synod: calling and ordaining a series of seminary graduates, each of whom served for a two-year grounding in pastoral ministry with further graduate study built in. As the fourth such assistant pastor I remember well my first day on the job. Pastor Geiseman sat me down for a talk which began, "There's one thing I want you to be clear about right away. . . ." I thought I knew what would follow: precautions against presumptuousness as a know-it-all seminary graduate eager to re-arrange well established practices, etc. Nothing of the sort. This is what he said: "We on the staff are up to our ears in the work and can't always see more of what the Lord calls us to do. You're a newcomer. You come with fresh eyes. Help us see what we haven't yet seen. Don't wait around. Speak up. We need you and the best you can bring." Then he added with a twinkle in his eye, "That's why we're paying you enormous amounts of money."

My two years lengthened out to eight years, due to his bouts with illness and other matters. His mentoring has blessed me more than I can express. I join with you today in thanking God for Otto Geiseman's extraordinary pastoral gifts which he shared so generously with us all. Together we give thanks and glory to God. O.A.G. would be the first to remind us that the glory belongs to God.

The freshness and beauty of God's love for us in Christ did not lose its luster throughout his forty-year ministry at Grace. That's what happens when the Holy Spirit keeps pastors humble in living the Gospel they preach and teach to others. When we would come to him with our troubles, large or small, he made time for us. He was not surprised or shocked by what he heard. He gave us wise counsel and seasoned understanding that was sound in the Law that exposes our sins and deeply rooted in the Gospel of Christ's saving love. In the pulpit, in the study, in hospitals, in homes, in jails, in railroad cars, planes, boats, and sometimes in bars, Otto Geiseman held the cross before people as the source of new life in God. That is the lasting image we'll carry from his ministry, the one he would most want us to cherish.

This is our prayer as we commend our beloved under-shepherd to the Chief Shepherd: "Thy will be done on earth as it is in heaven." In God's answer lies all we need now and all we can hope for in the tomorrows that lie ahead.

Who Will Follow?

October 3, 1976
Mark 8:34-35
F. Dean Lueking, Preacher

If any man would come after me, let him take up his cross and follow me. For whoever would save his life will lose it; and whoever loses his life for my sake and the gospel's will save it. (Mark 8:34-35)

The call to bear the cross laid upon the followers of Jesus. It is answered in many forms by Christians as this sermon illustrates. Current persecution of believers by totalitarian regimes in Asia, South America, and Africa is cited. The ordeal of enduring the accusation of being a teacher of false doctrine is another form of cross-bearing closer home laid upon Grace parishioner, Ralph Gehrke. The time for decision whether to remain in or to withdraw from the Lutheran Church–Missouri Synod was drawing closer; this sermon was preached just over one year before the September 1977 vote to leave was taken. What cross bearing is and how it becomes a hidden blessing of divine grace is what the sermon seeks to lift up as a mark of true discipleship.

Sacrifice. Self-denial. Cross-bearing.

These things belong to what being a Christian means. Are you, am I, ready to follow? We're wise not to answer too glibly. Cross-bearing goes against our natural inclination toward being comfortable and self-indulgent. Does putting that inclination first really prepare us for life in general, not to mention living as one who follows Jesus?

I thought of this recently when hearing a remark from a young physician who was attending a dying patient. He said that there's no reason why her pain should continue; the medical procedure being followed should eliminate it. Ivan Illich recent book, *Medical Nemesis* states that such thinking shows the deep crisis in medicine today—the commonly held idea that life should be pain free and that nothing can be learned from bearing it.

Against that, think of Winston Churchill telling the people of Great Britain at the outset of WWII that what lay ahead was blood, sweat, and tears—but that the sacrifice called for in enduring the Nazi menace would be worth it. He told the hard truth that held a hidden promise.

In a far deeper vein, bearing the cross that comes because we follow the Lord Jesus is saving because Jesus bore it for us before it was laid upon us. We cannot carry the cross he carried. For in that cross lay the weight of the world's sin, all the guilt and shame generated by our rebellious will, all the futility of thinking that "a God without wrath sent His Son without a cross into a world without sin" (Richard Niebuhr). Have no part in such a caricature of the Gospel of our salvation.

What, then, is cross-bearing? The late William Temple put it this way: "Cross bearing for Christians means that we choose to do or to suffer what apart from our love for Christ we should not choose to do or suffer." Plainly spoken: cross bearing is living by the costly grace of Jesus. It comes as a result of our baptism and life under the Holy Spirit. That means forgiving as we've been forgiven. Returning evil with good. Loving instead of hating. Confessing Jesus as Lord and having done with all that would replace him as first in the heart.

That fulfills your life and mine, not ruins it. Such cross-bearing, countercultural as it is, is finding the only life that finally matters. There is a real joy that comes from discipleship, a joy deeper than pleasure and more lasting than happiness.

Take heart, people of Grace, as you hear of cross-bearers of the faith in other parts of the world who live their witness under harsh circumstances of political tyranny.

In Korea, on both sides of the Iron Curtain there, Christians are jailed and harassed because they speak against tyranny in the name of the living Lord. In Chile, Argentina, and other countries in South America the same story is being lived out. A courageous Lutheran churchman, Helmut Frenz, has been banished from his native Chile for the past ten years because he has spoken out against the cruelty of injustice in that land. In Zimbabwe (formerly called Rhodesia) and Namibia (formerly South West Africa) there are Christians today who have been driven from their homes and jobs and live as refugees because they will not bow before authoritarian regimes that will not tolerate the justice that God calls for. I read last week of Christians of the Coptic Church in Egypt who suffer for the Gospel because of their refusal to convert to Islam. In too many places of the earth today there are people who endure confiscation of property, arrest without warrant, and detention without trial. Christians are among them.

Closer home, I must inform you that our fellow Grace member, Ralph Gehke, has endured thirteen years of charges of false doctrine made against him by Missouri Synod pastors who will not accept his plain confession of the biblical truth—the truth he has taught us in Bible classes, seminars, and retreats for years. Dr. Gehrke is not guilty of false doctrine. His calling on the Concordia Teachers College faculty is based on his fidelity to Christ and the Bible as God's inspired Word. His manner of life is exemplary as a humble, gifted, devoted servant of the Gospel. What he has been judged guilty of is his knowledge of how certain texts of the Old Testament have come down to us in their present form—not by magic—but by a process of transmission from one generation to another. We of Grace Church will stand by our brother. I want you to see the specific charges against him and hear his own confession of faith and loyalty to being a scholar in the church in a way that draws from the tradition of Martin Luther. A heavy cross is laid on Gehrke, whose entire lifetime of teaching the faith has been put under the cloud of suspicion and alleged heresy. That is no way to treat a gifted man of faith.

Even closer home, some of you know the cross of being the only practicing Christian in your marriage. That is a cross to bear. Some of you know the burden of caring for someone dear to you who suffers from chronic disease, or an emotional/mental disorder, or from old age. Some of you carry your Christian faith into your workplace and find that it does not make you popular among people who are grasping, shallow, and self-serving. That can mean denying yourself advancement or the questionable favors of compromising your basic Christian convictions.

So be it.

Here's a very short story that can help as you take up your cross and follow the Leader. A man came home from the last war with an empty coat sleeve. A tactless neighbor said, "I see you've lost your arm." The veteran answered firmly, "I didn't lose it. I gave it." His response was one more way of expressing the truth that "whoever would save his life will lose it, and whoever loses his life for my sake finds it." Amen.

The Testimony of the Heart
Trinity IV

July 22, 1971
Romans 10:1
F. Dean Lueking, Preacher

Brothers and sisters, my heart's desire and prayer to God for them is that they may be saved. (Romans 10:1)

This sermon, more than any other I preached through the turbulent 1970s, was consequential for the Grace decision to withdraw from the Synod in 1977. It was preached four years prior to that action, on July 22, 1973, immediately after my return from the LCMS convention in New Orleans. At that meeting a document written by the Synod President, Jacob A.O. Preus, was declared—by a narrow vote—to be binding on the faith and conscience of all members of the Synod. The dire effects of that action were on my mind as I preached the Romans 10:10 text. Never before had I received such a strong response to a sermon, none of it neutral, most of it positive, some of it heatedly negative.

In three weeks from today, it will be twenty-nine years since I knelt at the Grace altar for ordination into the office of the holy ministry. I publicly vowed to conform my ministry to the authority of the inspired Holy Scriptures as the sole norm for faith and doctrine and the three ecumenical creeds and the Lutheran confessions as faithful witnesses to the authority of the biblical faith.

Today I repeat that vow in your presence: "I believe in the power of the Gospel to create and sustain the faith whereby we are saved, and in the Holy Scriptures, the Creeds, and the Lutheran Confessions as the standard for my preaching, teaching, and pastoral care for you."

Why do I do this now?

Because—and this I say with much sadness—it has been declared insufficient.

This happened last week in a convention of the Lutheran Church–Missouri Synod, our denominational home since 1902. In an unprecedented action, by a majority vote of 562-455, after raucous debate by opposing parties, a document known as a "Statement of Scriptural and Confessional Principles" was declared binding on the faith and conscience of the several million members of the LCMS.

It is right for a synodical convention to hear matters of doctrinal importance, to speak together in brotherly care in applying them to our life and work, to make every effort to admonish, reprove, encourage, and build each other up in the holy faith handed down from the prophets and apostles. That is the precious, sacred work of the Holy Spirit—to bind the faith-filled conscience to the saving truth of Holy Scripture.

But it is wrong for synodical convention delegates to make a doctrinal statement of human authorship binding on the Christian conscience of any believer. That is disastrously wrong!

With a heavy heart I tell you this: our church body has experienced a hostile takeover. In the world of business you know what that means; one power group outmuscles another to gain control. That has now happened in the church, our church.

It began in 1969 when one party of disaffected pastors and laity gained control of the Synod presidency through shameful politicizing that ousted the incumbent, Dr. Oliver Harms, and seated a newcomer to the office, Dr. Jacob Preus, whose announced agenda was to rid the synod of alleged false doctrine. It has progressed through the past five years of groundless accusations against the faculty of Concordia Seminary, St. Louis—the faculty that formed me theologically and scores of other pastors like me. Now that the Preus statement has been elevated to its new authority as the measuring stick of who is sound and who is false as a Lutheran Christian, the witch hunt is on. Faculties of the synod's other schools will be interrogated, including nearby Concordia Teachers College, and our own respected Grace members who teach the faith to future teachers in parochial schools of the church.

What is all this about?

It has been framed by the Preus party as a dispute between liberals and conservatives, a kind of theological mirror image, if you will, of the political liberal/conservative debacle that plagues our nation currently.

That's a false reading. Liberal theology—in the sense of denial of God the Creator created all things visible and invisible, who sent his only Son Jesus to die and rise again for our salvation, who sent the Holy Spirit who calls, gather, enlightens, and sanctifies the whole Christian church on earth—is not found in our church body.

What is found is loveless bickering, slanderous accusations, and the failure in all of us to speak the truth in love. I find all this terribly hard to say to you, dear people of Grace, but I must tell it like it is. Bear with me, people of Grace, especially you who find all this puzzling, offensive, and out of place in a sermon. I assure you there will be open meetings, well publicized and well ordered to give all sides a hearing. We will not be obsessed with Synodical controversies nor will we sidestep our responsibility to face them.

Take a deep breath, now, and turn from these worrisome matters of the head to the salutary matters of the heart where faith, hope, and love abide. We have a text, a word from the Lord, to hear and to heed: "For man believes with his heart and so is justified, and he confesses with his lips and so is saved" (Romans 10:10).

Man believes with his heart. How directly that speaks to us! The biblical meaning of heart is not that exotic muscle in the center of your chest. The heart is our spiritual center, that deep, inward capacity of the soul where God's working, not man's, prevails. St. Paul teaches us that with his heart, man believes. Believes what? That God our gracious heavenly Father has made us His own beloved children through Jesus His Son, who took upon himself our sins and suffered the damning judgment of God that we deserve. Jesus is risen. He is exalted to the right hand of God's power. With the Father, Jesus has sent upon us the Holy Spirit to dwell in your heart and in mine and in every believer.

The most revered theologian of the LCMS, who was president of the synod and president of Concordia Seminary, Franz Pieper wrote these words in his *Christian Dogmatics*:

> Christ has commissioned neither some one person (pope, prince, governor, president, etc.) nor a college of persons (bishops, pastors, boards of directors, consistories, parliaments, conferences, synods, councils, etc.) to decide and ordain ecclesiastical matters for the Church

in any way binding the conscience. . . When they do, this is not a Christian Church but a papistic position, because in the Christian Church God's Word is the only authority and all Christians are to remain responsible directly to God for all they believe and do (cf. pp. 423-433).

What are we now to do as people who believe with our hearts, and what are we to confess with our lips so that we might be saved?

We must speak the truth in love. In New Orleans we saw and heard little or no speaking the truth in love but a great deal of divisive speech propelled by raw power.

We must not walk out on the whole mess in denial of the crisis at hand.

We must hold open forums in the congregation in which all can participate.

We must not withhold our support of faithful synodical workers here and overseas.

To our young men considering the pastoral ministry, don't give up that hope.

All of us, pray God in all earnestness for his healing grace to heal our divided church.

Much there is that is unknown and unsettling as we look ahead. Here are words of T.S. Eliot that serve us well:

> If we take the widest and wisest view of a Cause,
> There is no such thing as a Lost Cause
> Because there is no such thing as a Gained Cause.
> We fight for lost causes
> Because we know that our defeat and dismay
> May be the preface to our successor's victory,
> Though that victory itself will be temporary:
> We fight rather to keep something alive
> Than in expectation that anything will triumph.

This, fellow Christians, is what we fight for, to keep something alive—the testimony of the heart.

In Newness of Life

Trinity VI

July 29, 1973
Romans 6:18-23
F. Dean Lueking, Preacher

And that you, having been set free from sin, have become slaves of righteousness. I am speaking in human terms because of your natural limitations. For just as you once presented your members as slaves to impurity and to greater and greater iniquity, so now present your members as slaves to righteousness for sanctification. When you were slaves of sin, you were free in regard to righteousness. So what advantage did you then get from the things of which you now are ashamed? The end of those things is death. But now that you have been freed from sin and enslaved to God, the advantage you get is sanctification. The end is eternal life. For the wages of sin is death, but the free gift of God is eternal life in Christ Jesus our Lord. (Romans 6:18-23)

Before there was Grace Lutheran Church there was Grace Lutheran School. The latter was founded in 1896, the former in 1904. In the years since there has been a consistent effort to keep the unity of congregation and school as one ministry united in mission outreach and mutual upbuilding in faith. This sermon from 1973 begins with an example of that unity at work. Later in the sermon there is an illustration of how a 1973 event that marked a highlight of the drug culture in America contrasted with the way of life baptismal grace brings about. I left it to the congregation then (and to the sermon reader now) to determine whether the comparison works. At least it was and is an effort to place the eternal good of baptism alongside a widely known event of the time. It's striking, isn't it, how the latter has faded while the former has not and will not.

A couple well into their 60s came in for a visit recently to inquire about the possibility of enrolling a third grader and a sixth grader in Grace Lutheran School. What was unusual about this inquiry was that the couple is Roman Catholic and the children were not their own but their God-children. The natural parents of the 8-year-old girl and the boy of 11 have divorced and abandoned their children. When the children were baptized some years ago, this Roman Catholic couple meant it as their baptismal sponsors when promising to see to the children's well-being, spiritually and physically. Baptism was not regarded as a pious gesture but taken with a holy seriousness as the entrance into the new life with Jesus as Lord and membership in his family which includes all baptized Christians as brothers and sisters in faith.

These youngsters will be in our school this fall. Our Grace School principal assures that a place will be found for them. All of this is best seen as having the Sacrament of Baptism at its heart and center. Baptism puts us into newness of life, life here on earth as well as the coming life in heaven. We need that reminder, again and again we need it so that we avoid the blight of taking it for granted or demeaning it as having little or nothing to do with the two children named above, their baptismal sponsors, and us as their fellow baptized brothers and sisters in Christ.

Strong Words on Baptism

The text for today's sermon on baptism is from Paul's letter to the Christians in Rome: "We were buried therefore with Christ by baptism into death, so that as Christ was raised from the dead by the glory of the Father, we too might walk in newness of life. . . ."

The words call to mind not the lace of a baptismal gown handed down in the family from previous baptisms. Nor whose turn it is to be God-parents. Nor who will host the family dinner after church. Nor even the lovely sight of an infant presented at the font for the ceremony of baptism. All are fine and wonderful things that are part of our associations with baptism.

Death by drowning is not a part of that mental picture. That is the dominant image of the text and it is terrifically strong, even shockingly so. It's not out of place but takes us to the heart of what takes place when we are baptized. We go down into cold watery death, the death that is sin's last and foremost assault. We go down into that death with Christ, united with him in his death. The words are jarring, I repeat, and meant to be so.

What Dies in Us?

What dies in us is what sin gave birth to in us. Above all, willful pride that blinds us to how we miss the mark and fail to measure up to God's holy will. What dies in us is stubborn resistance to love him with all our heart and the neighbor as ourselves. What dies in us is petty gossip, worry about money, stinginess in sharing, and pre-occupation with what to wear and how young we look.

Right at this point I hear a voice within me mocking what I've just said. It asks, "If all that dies in baptism, why do baptized Christians still gossip, worry, and obsess over clothes and appearance?" If we're told that we've drowned to sin by being joined with Christ, why does sin keep bobbing up to haunt us again and again?

Dying to Sin, Day by Day

While baptism brings us to newness of life in Christ—who gave his life on the cross for us and was raised on the third day for us—our unity with him by faith means that we die daily to sin. It's faith in action that brings this about. The best way to start the day is to remember your baptism, seek God's grace in prayer, and live out the day as one who is fighting the good fight of faith. Dying daily to sin is a more radical, a more biblical, way of saying that living our baptismal identity puts us on the path of discipleship with an eye on our resistance to it.

If you have a clearer way of putting it in your own words, please do so. Dying to sin and rising in baptismal grace to newness of life, day in and day out, can be expressed in many ways. Take hold of the way you can understand it, live it, and share it. We've got plenty of opposition both from within and without. The daily news stories describing what humans can do to humans in this year of our Lord, 1973, is starkly fearful in many aspects. And we've all got enough depressing news of how we're doing on the inside. The daily media and our own inside press is not what inspires and guides us in newness of life.

Born Again, and Again, and Again

Our baptismal covenant with the Lord Jesus delivers to us what our Savior has first done for us, made us children of God. When asked if you've been born again, answer Yes. If asked further about when and where, speak of your baptism. Do you know that date, that time, that place? It's more important than your birthday as your second birth day. Talk of being born again isn't widespread among us Lutherans. That's because the phrase has been taken over by Christians who insist on a dramatic time and place when "we took Jesus into our heart" or some similar way of putting it. But that places the emphasis on us, as though we as the newly-born are the initiators of rebirth.

Keep first things first, God's opening up his arms to receive us via the cross which his beloved Son carried for us. The resurrection of the Lord, his ascension to the Father's right hand of rule, his sending of the Holy Spirit through the Gospel—this is first and foremost. It's true whether we feel religious or not in any given moment. It's true when our faith and trust sag. It's true when the odds against it look insurmountable.

The Gospel, Christ's saving work for us, is the good news for our bad situation, and that of others. In human words which point clearly to Jesus the Savior, God puts his power to forgive, renew, and reconcile us. He puts his power—of all things—into a word we can speak. In fallible human language. Is that so odd? When two people speak their vows at the wedding altar, they speak human words meant to bind them in lifelong fidelity and love. When we speak the Pledge of Allegiance, we're speaking words which identify us as citizens in a democracy for which many have given their lives. When someone tells the winner of the Irish sweepstakes they've won a pile of money, they usually jump up and down with glee. "You have been united with Christ in a death like his and raised with him to newness of life!" is the news that makes the heart sing, stirs hope of new beginnings, delivers from the worst, and gives us our place in the new family of God. There's no better news. Receive it again today and cherish it above all things.

Getting High on Feelings

Last week in Woodstock, New York, more than 600,000 rock music fans gathered for a weekend of non-stop music. For many of them, according to news reports, it was a drug-saturated couple of days, with their feelings pumped up to a non-stop high. On the subject of feelings but in a much different way, Martin Luther was a keenly attuned to his feelings. He knew well those spiritual flatlands, periods made bleak by doubt whether the Lord really accepted him as he knew himself to be, in thrall to sin. During that year in his life when his political overseer put him in the Wartburg Castle for protective custody, he spent many lonely hours. When anxious, he would take a piece of chalk from his desk and write, "I have been baptized." He would take those four words to heart and apply them to his fears. Whether your write them on a table top or not, it's a good thing to remember your baptism. Remember that God has called you by name. You are his. You have his Gospel promise to hang onto. Hang onto it.

Our baptismal assurance that our lives have worth to God and meaning to ourselves deserves attention in our time in which much attention is paid to our human senses, especially our feelings. They are, after all, God's good creation. They must not be thought of as otherwise. The problem occurs when feelings are put first, above faith, good sense, and the deeper satisfaction of the Christ-like life.

The Greater Gathering, the Permanent Blessing

Again and again, the congregation is where Christians all over the world build one another in faith through acts of serving with lots of stewardship, befriending and opening doors to strangers.

We're among them. Not as the gathering of the perfect by any means. Right now Grace Church is going through a demanding time in our relationship to our denomination. But that strain cannot dim the joy or replace the goodness of living our baptismal covenant together.

Here's something special to do this week. If you are a baptismal sponsor, take time to write a note or make a phone call to your God-child. In words that are altogether your own, tell them that you're thinking of them and that your prayers include them. I have God-children; I'll do what I'm suggesting to you.

And as a baptized person yourself, think of your own God-parent(s). Thank the heavenly Father for them in your prayers this week. If it is possible, contact them in some way to let them know that you are glad for their spiritual role in your life. That communication can get no better than by quoting from the Romans 6:4 words of Paul that lift this sacrament of entrance to the full dignity and splendor that it deserves.

May the peace of God which passes all understanding keep your hearts and minds in Christ Jesus.

Ready to Lead
Installation of Gerald Koenig, Principal

September 18, 1980
Luke 16:10
F. Dean Lueking, *Preacher*

Whoever is faithful in a very little is faithful also in much;
and whoever is dishonest in a very little is dishonest also in
much. (Luke 16:10)

Ministry in a congregation with a Christian school functions best when pastors and teachers work together as partners in the Gospel, called to show a collegial spirit of mutual love and support in serving the congregation and school. I inherited that spirit of teamwork from my predecessor, Otto Geiseman, and the Grace School principal, Victor Waldschmidt. In this sermon, preached at the installation of Gerald Koenig as the eighth principal in the eighty-three-year history of the school, together with the installation of our new teachers on the Grace Lutheran School faculty, the theme of a unified ministry of church and school stands out. By incorporating their installation in a regular Sunday morning service the oneness of the Grace ministry of congregation and school was all the more evident.

What's Behind That Wall?

A visitor at this service might wonder what's on the other side of the chancel wall. Today is a good moment for all of us to know what goes on each day of the week, 176 days a year, behind the chancel wall to the south of this sanctuary.

Grace School goes on there.

That means 270 children, from junior kindergarten through the eighth grade—children of varied interests and talents, of different races, and in more recent years we can add that some children come to our school from Muslim and Hindu backgrounds. And some from little or no religious backgrounds at all. All are welcome. All are received as marvels of God's creation. Most important of all, all are loved. With a waiting list of eighty boys and girls, we're serving all our building will accommodate. Grace School is a vital partner with Grace Church in the one ministry the Lord gives us. We're unified in what we do together.

Integral to Our Whole Ministry

Grace School is not something separate from our whole parish family. These children and the full staff of their teachers and support staff are integral to our purpose of teaching and preaching the Gospel of Christ. The way in which we as pastors and teachers love, respect, and care for each other as members of a unified staff gives integrity to what we do together in serving school and congregation. That means we forgive each other as we have been forgiven by our Savior. We encourage each other as people to whom the Holy Spirit has given unique gifts. We comfort each other in times of sorrow. We rejoice together as friends who enjoy each other's company. Where we fail to do these things, our common ministry is weakened. It shows. We can't hide. But because we live together by the forgiveness of sins we don't pretend perfection. We're not special, not above or below or distant from you, the people of Grace congregation and Grace School. And we're all here today on a quite special Sunday to welcome a new principal and four new teachers into their high calling at Grace Lutheran School.

Grace School predates Grace congregation. In 1897 a group of families, then members of St. John's Lutheran Church in Forest Park, asked for and received permission to build a one-room frame school house on the nearby corner of Augusta and Belleforte in Oak Park. Five years later Grace Lutheran Church was chartered. It's good for us to remember that the congregation grew from the school beginnings. Without the prior formation of the school there would have been no congregation. The reverse is true. Grace School could not operate without the loyal support and enlightened commitment of all 1,750 of us in the congregation.

A New Leader, Ready to Lead

We install a new principal today. Gerald L. Koenig is the eighth principal in this eighty-third year of the school's history. We also install four new teachers on our faculty. It's truly a day of celebration and thanksgiving, as well as rededication to the high calling of giving children a basis in their educational journey.

As in all aspects of the church's ministry, the ministry of Christian education takes leadership. We are here to say to you, Gerald, our friend and brother, "You are ready to lead." We have that confidence. We share it with you.

What Criterion for Leadership?

When is a man or woman ready to lead? Answers vary in different sectors of life. In our democratic system of government, a person is ready to lead when elected. An heir-apparent in a family business takes over when the designated chronological age is reached. Or when a high-level funeral occurs.

But in the work of Christ's church, readiness to lead comes through a special criterion for which there is no substitute. Jesus says it this way in today's Gospel reading: ". . . he who is faithful in a very little is faithful also in much . . ." (Luke 16:10).

Especially with Children

Faithfulness in little things prepares one for larger roles of leadership, and few people get a clearer picture of that than teachers in schools where the Christian faith is the heartbeat of all that goes on.

Prisca Bretscher, you take on your calling today as teacher of kindergarten children. Little things have to do with little people, our four and five year olds who are entering a whole new world when they step into a school building for the first time. Just to swing open that big door is a big accomplishment. I've seen the worried look on their faces when they find that door shut on a blustery morning and their relief as a helping hand shows up. You know from nearly a decade of experience what it means to help young children to use scissors, to tell time, to learn the alphabet, to get the right snow boot on the right foot. We don't start school at any other point than the beginning point, and young children seem to sense if a teacher is with them in love or merely putting up with them. Faithfulness in little things sets the tone for the learning experience for years to come. Prisca, what a high calling you have with us!

William Schwarz, you have charge of our learning center. Your work puts you in a close connection with all of our school children by means of opening up to them the boundless horizons of reading—what it means to a child not only to learn to read but to learn to love reading! Words flash across the most important screen they have—that of their mind and imagination—where images are conjured up and holy truths are played out. Words unlock the experiences of past ages, the wonders of nature, the mysteries of science, the beauty of language. Our children, like all kids in our part of the world, spend at least five hours in front of television sets daily, so the experts tell us. Scooby-do and Bugs Bunny resonate more in their ears than most would admit. Happy is the learning center director who moves young minds beyond the confining images of the screen to the endless horizons of their own lively minds.

Christine Tierney, your sixth grade classroom is a launching pad for children who are getting more and more into integrating all kinds of previous years of learning. Spelling and religion, social studies and math—these tools are getting sharpened in the critically important year you teach them. I remember my own sixth grade peaks and valleys. I spent much of that year not fully sure that 9 times 7 was 63. Does that kind of thing still exist? Sixth grade boys and girls are growing physically as well as mentally and spiritually in the year you have them under your wing. Assure them, day in and day out, that Jesus' love is what makes them understand, accept, and take good care of themselves. They're no longer little children but on their way into that bewildering, marvelous time known as pre-adolescence. You have a high calling, Christine, and faithfulness in little things is the key to your leading them to the greater things into which they are growing.

Gloria Hillert, your eighth grade assignment is centered on the science side of the final year of their Grace School education. They begin to work with test tubes and chemical vials. They are introduced by you into the micro-world of particles which form the elements with which we live and by which we live. All that can be opened up as a realm that created itself, or it can be introduced as one facet of the Creator's handiwork. Reverence for God is the beginning of wisdom. That key truth is at the heart of your work and all our work as a Christian school. You help not to scorn or suspect science as an enemy of faith, but to respect and be curious about things scientific because it is all God's laboratory where he is still at work in marvelous ways.

Christ our Savior, who loved you and gave himself for you, makes you ready to lead because you've first learned to follow as his disciple. He is with you and for you—the cross he endured is the sign of the greatness of the love in which he holds you in His heart, fills up what you lack, and keeps your commitment to children strong and healthy. We parents really appreciate you because we have no more precious things to put into your hands than our children. We respect you. We love you. We pray for you. Our school is blessed to have you.

That's why this installation belongs in the Sunday worship where all of us gather. The Spirit of God makes us all partners with you. We do not have a private school here on the corner of Bonnie Brae and Division. School and congregation are under one Lord, one faith, one calling. And it's a great thing that half of our children come from families beyond Grace Church who reflect the larger community of God's people. All the more important to us are children with little or no spiritual foundation. We all are here for all of the children and their families. And the whole school is part and parcel of the whole congregation we call Grace.

It makes a difference, this being faithful in little things as the prerequisite for leadership in larger things. This is especially true when serving children.

Here are two stories which show what happens when faithfulness in little things is not there. And when it is.

Seventy years ago, in a Yugoslavian village, a youngster helping to serve Mass accidentally spilled some communion wine in the chancel of the parish church. The priest admonished him gruffly, telling him to get out of the church. He got out. And stayed out. That little boy's name is Josip Broz, also known as Marshall Tito. His Marxist life of leadership was lived in conspicuous distance from the church and the Christian faith. At roughly the same time, a somewhat similar thing took place. A lad, not quite free from nervousness in a Sunday Mass, made a similar mistake. The priest put a fatherly arm around the boy's shoulder, winked at him, and said he would make a fine priest one day. The boys' name was Fulton Sheen, and the priest's prediction came true indeed.

It makes a difference, doesn't it—being faithful in little things which lead to faithfulness in greater things. Nothing ever happens without some sort of previous preparation. The temptation to take shortcuts around that truth is strong, but the results are disastrous. Resist that temptation! Our day in the world and our time in the church are filled with sad examples. But there are shining instances of the power of the Lord's truth coming through. We are here to be humble as we ask for God's grace to keep us faithful. And we're here with gratitude that we can be part of what's happening here today.

What might your calling to leadership, your faithfulness in larger things look like, Gerry and teachers who are installed today, years down the line? Instilling a love for God and a love of learning in children, being partners with us parents in setting a Christian example are highly promising. Building a sense of justice, honesty, duty, responsibility, care for others—especially those different from us—is a holy work. Helping children to love learning, be intellectually curious, and well founded in character is a calling second to none. It means not just stuffing young heads with facts but nurturing young minds toward wisdom. Surely these are the "larger things" which call for faithfulness, for continued growth in learning as good teachers, for satisfaction in your work, and for appreciation for the gifts you apply as teachers.

We are with you and for you. Grace School is just what the name implies: grace! May it abound in God's favor, in growth in learning and in reverence for God among the children who are well served.

We have a new leader and a quartet of four new teachers for Grace School today. They're ready. God be praised. Amen.

A Gift from God
Wilfred F. Kruse Funeral Sermon

January 3, 1983
1 Corinthians 12:4-7
F. Dean Lueking, Preacher

Now there are varieties of gifts but the same Spirit; and there are varieties of service but the same Lord; and there are varieties of the working, but it is the same God who inspires them all in every one. To each is given the manifestation of the Spirit for the common good.
(1 Corinthians 12:4-7)

This sermon belongs in this book as a testimony to the close ties between Grace Lutheran Church and Concordia Teachers College—now Concordia University Chicago. It was preached at the funeral of Dr. Wilfred Kruse on January 3, 1983. He was a long-time faculty member and academic dean at the college, as well as a long-time and much respected member of Grace Lutheran Church. His funeral sermon included testimony to his role as a bridge uniting the two communities in ways of mutual benefit to each. This needs remembering, especially after those close ties were strained following the 1977 withdrawal of Grace from the LCMS, an action that Dr. Kruse supported after struggling with its personal implications as well as broader impact upon both the congregation and the college.

We come together in this church today still feeling the shock of the sudden death of Prof. Wilfred Kruse, who sat in his regular church pew place for New Year's Eve worship only four evenings ago. We all feel it. And all of us reach out to you family members who feel his loss most deeply. In the grimness of death, even as in the goodness of life, we turn to our God who is our refuge and strength for comfort in our loss and for hope as we look ahead.

What a gifted man he was!

In making that statement, and in turning over in our minds the many memories and associations with him, we are not so much speaking a eulogy (which would make him frown) as we are speaking in tribute to the Holy Spirit, the giver of all the varied gifts that made Butch Kruse the gifted man he was.

The Apostle Paul weaves together a tapestry of marvelous truths in this text. Notice how two words recur—varieties and same. God made us in his image in such a way that each of us is unique. Each possesses particular qualities of mind and spirit. Yet all that variety is the work of the one Spirit, the same Lord. Dr. Kruse's eighty-two years of life is a wonderful testimony to the rich diversity and yet singular quality of the gifts God gave him.

The Gift above Every Gift

The best gift God gave Wilfred Kruse is the one that has not been touched, tarnished, or destroyed by death. God's saving love in his Son, our crucified and risen Lord Jesus, is the gift that did not fail him as his human life left him with cruel suddenness. The Savior who loved us and gave himself for us has put down death, withdrawn its sting, and makes good on his promise to be the Good Shepherd who leads his own through the valley and shadow of death to be with him in the house of the Lord forever. "Christ is risen, he is risen indeed" is the Easter shout we raise to the resurrected Lord. In the quiet of our saddened hearts today, let there be that calming assurance: Christ is risen—for Wilfred Frederick Kruse. He is risen indeed, and keeps the beloved husband and father, churchman and friend, safely in his care.

The Gospel is good news of what Jesus our Lord does in the face of the bad news of the damage sin has done. The cross is the sign of a costly victory won at Calvary so long ago. There the cross stands—above the casket before us today—with hope, comfort, and peace for your hearts and mine.

Life Built on the Solid Rock

Wilfred Kruse's life had a solid foundation. His baptism into the Lord's family was its cornerstone. To be sure, his family genes and inherited traits all play a part in who and what he was. But it goes deeper than that. What stands out so clearly in his years is connected with words like "integrity," "soundness," "dependability"—and any other word that calls to mind the granite-like quality of the life Butch lived. For so many of us he was a father figure. When the need arose for real discernment and sound judgment in matters that count, it was so natural to turn to him. Even those who might not have always agreed with him respected him. In no sense was he swayed by the popularity of whichever opinion was in vogue at the moment, nor was he willing to concede principle to expediency. He strove mightily to be the Lord's man, as a husband, father, faculty professor, and congregation member.

Because he was clear about God as the giver of his gifts, he gained a well-earned reputation as one worth consulting when wisdom was needed. "Ask what Prof. Kruse thinks" has been an unspoken rule that many have followed in our parish journey through church conflict. That has blessed me as pastor even as it has blessed you as parishioners. On a much broader plane of family life, you Kruse family members have seen that grace of good humor played out again and again. He's the only man I know who could tell jokes in four languages.

Loving God with the Mind

Another gift that comes quickly to mind when thinking of his life is that of a keen mind.

Not only did he participate in conventions, committee work, and much else in the church for over fifty years, but he could tell us on what page of what volume the report about it was recorded! Carl Halter's fitting words of tribute to his colleague catch the point well: meticulous, detailed, exact. If a thing was worth doing at all, it was worth doing with the precision and best effort of the mind as well as body and spirit. Wilfred Kruse helped us see the virtue of loving God with the mind! He kept developing it through his graduate education endeavors. He applied in invaluably over the decades of his service at Concordia Teachers College—both in Seward, Nebraska, and here in River Forest.

Not many Concordia Seminary, St. Louis, Missouri, graduates of the Class of 1923 went on to graduate school to major in mathematics, chemistry, and the sciences. He did so, aware that he was given a keen mind for the purpose of developing and applying it for the good of the hundreds and thousands of students he taught. I should not fail to mention the lively interest he had in Purdue University football and the great fun he had in analyzing the prospects for the coming season of the Boilermakers.

I bear witness to the vital link between Concordia College and Grace congregation Prof. Kruse has been. It's made him a bridge between campus and congregation. There is no better way to honor his memory than to keep building and sustaining that bridge-like connection between Grace and Concordia. It is done as we put into practice the relationships built upon respect, mutual honor, and Christian good will. This would be dear to Dr. Kruse's heart since he had a role beyond all others in building and sustaining the bridge that binds our two communities together. During his many years as the academic dean of the College he was also the assistant pastor in Grace congregation. I remember his participation in my ordination service in August 1954 and in many a church meeting since. Always with blessing. Not once with regret.

Loving Family, Beloved by Family

Our Lord Jesus came to us who have been orphaned by sin to restore us to God's family, and to make our earthly families a sign of that eternal family. "I came that they might have life, and have it more abundantly," Jesus said. And St. Paul explained what that can mean by calling us to cherish "whatever is true, honorable, just, pure, lovely, gracious, and excellent" (Philippians 4:18 ff.).

To be in Christ is to relish life.

You, Natale, and the daughters and close family members know that best of all, for you have lived it in the Kruse household. Cherish all the dear associations and happy times of life with Butch Kruse, knowing that they will only grow in blessing as the future unfolds. Those memorable days at Lake James, or on the tennis court in earlier years, the golf course later on, and in the poker games that made him the hard man to beat—and countless other memories that are yours: hold them close. Cherish them gratefully. They will mellow with the passing of the years.

Tender Healing for Your Wounded Hearts

To all who sorely miss Prof. Kruse, especially his close family, turn your wounded hearts over to the healing Lord. "Neither death nor life, nor anything else in all creation shall be able to separate us from the love of God in Christ Jesus our Lord" (Romans 8:39 ff.). That is the strong word of our tender Lord that will fortify you as you pass through the coming days, one day at a time. We have this treasure of life in earthen vessels, don't we! How earthen the vessel of life is has come home to us in the recent days. But the recent days must be seen in the frame of the eternal day of resurrection and eternal life through the Lord who has gone ahead to prepare a place for us.

That gift will not fade nor fail. Christ will see us through, beyond this life, to the promised reunion with all the faithful of all time and place. That includes Wilfred Kruse, whom we commend to God today.

May the peace of God which passes all understanding keep your hearts and minds in Christ Jesus.

Our Debt to Israel

February 6, 1961
Matthew 5:17
F. Dean Lueking, *Preacher*

Do not think that I have come to abolish the law or the prophets; I have come not to abolish but to fulfill. (Matthew 5:17)

Friendships with neighboring rabbis grew during my pastoral years at Grace. I consciously sought those personal ties as a natural outgrowth of the common roots Christians and Jews share in the Old Testament Scriptures. I encouraged cooperative participation between Grace and nearby synagogue members in such community endeavors as improving race relations, eliminating red lining in real estate practices, and publicly opposing marches through our towns by the American Nazi Party. This sermon brought that witness into focus from the words of Jesus in his Sermon on the Mount. When its title appeared on the bulletin board in front of the Grace entrance, a rabbi friend noticed it and expressed curiosity about what it meant. I sent him a copy of this sermon as a sign of my appreciation of his inquiry. I should add that in the more recent years of Israel's unconscionable occupation of Palestine, an act that I actively oppose, the previous decades of close ties with neighboring rabbis have been tested. To deny that testing would be to undermine the integrity of my respect for the founding principles of the modern State of Israel. We must live with that tension and work toward its just resolution as the finest mark of friendship.

These words of our Lord from his Sermon on the Mount lead to an important truth for all Christians to remember. It speaks of our debt to Israel. Not a financial debt to the current State of Israel, of course, but our debt in the sense that God made a covenant with Abraham and his children and thus called into being those whom we call Israelites. We are people of the new covenant God made with us Gentiles through Jesus his Son. God did not nullify his promise to his Israelite children whom we call Jews. That's the point of Jesus' word: "Think not that I came to abolish the law and the prophets; I have not come to abolish but to fulfill them."

Jesus addressed those words to this problem that had arisen among his Jewish hearers. Many of the things that he proclaimed in his Sermon on the Mount shocked and offended them. They took issue with Jesus as one who broke all ties with the sacred covenant first with Abraham and confirmed at Sinai. By no means! Jesus declared. He did not preach and teach a new God or another God. He placed himself directly in the long line of the patriarchs not as their neighbor but the Messiah, the fulfiller to whom they had pointed and for whom they had prepared the way.

In the light of this text, my dear fellow Lutherans, we are all Jews. I mean this. We owe our heritage as New Testament Christians to God's chosen people according to his covenant with Abraham. It is a debt of gratitude. Why? Because they heard the word of God and kept it. They were not Christians. They lived long before Jesus was born. Yet they took their place in the line of those who lived by God's gracious promise. What did they do that puts us in their debt? Listen to this summary:

> . . . through faith they conquered kingdoms, enforced justice, received promises, stopped the mouths of lions, quenched raging fires . . . some were tortured, refusing to accept release . . . others suffered mocking and scourging, chains and imprisonment. They were stoned, they were sawn in two, they were killed by the sword; they went about in skins of sheep and goats, destitute, afflicted, ill-treated—of whom the world was not worthy, wandering over deserts and mountains, and in dens and caves of the earth (Hebrews 11:33-38).

Little wonder, then, that our Lord Jesus said so emphatically that he did not come to abolish the law and prophets—they are part of his plan of salvation for the world. We can no more rid ourselves of our link with them in the family of faith than we can rid ourselves of our own grandparents and cousins in our earthly families. Who would want to do that? Here is the greatest of all reasons we cherish our debt to Israel—our Lord Jesus Christ was a Jew, an Israelite.

It is a bitter irony, then, when Christians abandon our link to our forbears in the covenant line of God's mighty works. When that happens, it is Abraham, Moses, David, Ruth, Esther, Sarah, Hosea, Isaiah, and Jeremiah that we cut off from ourselves. There are country clubs in our time that would put a NOT WELCOME sign out if any of these would apply. There are social clubs and campus organizations that still bar Jews. Far worse, we live with the memory of the holocaust in WWII that took six million Jewish lives as victims of vicious Nazi ideology built upon the cornerstone of anti-Semitism.

Scorning faithful Jews is sinful. It is an act of defiance against the living God. Have no part in it whatsoever! We are Gentiles and have this to keep in mind; we are a "wild olive branch" grafted on to the main trunk of the tree, as Paul teaches (Romans 4:17—look it up). We are by nature strangers to God's covenant, included solely because of his mercy (Ephesians 2:10—look that one up, too). How can we act as though we owned God and his covenant and there are no Jews who are welcome? That's blasphemy.

A year ago I attended a lecture at our neighboring West Suburban Har Zion Synagogue. The speaker, a Christian, happened to mention that I had said publicly in an article that pitifully few Christians spoke up in behalf of Jews during the Nazi time in Germany. After the speaker had finished, a man strode resolutely to the speaker and said, "You stated that some Christians protested. There were two, Martin Niemoeller and Probst Grueber!" This man had lost all his family to the gas ovens. Whenever he heard the word "Christian" he thought of all those who looked the other way and played it safe. Yes, his estimate of only two Christians in all of Germany who stood up for the Jews was inadequate. But in large part he was correct, tragically. It was Dietrich Bonhoeffer, the Lutheran pastor who did stand up publicly for the Jews and paid for it with his life, who also said: "Only those Christians who stood up for the Jews can sing the hymns of Easter with a clear conscience." Those are strong words. They are true.

It is never hard to uncover the underlying currents of bias against Jews, nor is it difficult to hear stereotypes of Jews as slick with money, drivers of hard bargains, clannish folks who think of themselves as superior. If Jews are to be properly chastised, let Jews do that necessary work.

We belong to a Savior who reveals God's law, to be sure, by which are sins are exposed and for which we are called to penitence. We belong to a Savior who above all suffered for our sins and delivered us from the everlasting doom that we deserve. Through Jesus' death and resurrection we are made members of God's people! We have our place. The Gospel is our joy and treasure. In possessing it as our joy and grandest treasure we cannot but share it, with everyone—Jew and Gentile alike. Such witnessing calls for the greatest care and wisdom.

What can we make of the fact that great numbers of Jews whom we love and respect do not join us in confessing Jesus as God's only Son, and Savior and Lord of us all? Now we are face to face with one of the greatest mysteries of our faith. It is this: Israel—faithful Jews—carry on as witnesses to God's original covenant. They are still beloved of God for the sake of his covenant. His chosen people, the Jews, survive and shall ever survive. We march along as Gentile Christians, people of the new covenant in Christ. We do not have that mystery figured out. We live with it until the last day when this mystery will be unfolded at last.

Meanwhile we have much to do that calls for our working together. I begin with friendship. Every Christian should have a close friend who is Jewish. I have had that blessing from childhood on. It matters. Seek such friendships and tend them carefully. And think of the enrichment of life Jews give us. It's impossible to imagine the arts, music, letters, government, commerce, education, etc. Many of us have the benefit of skilled Jewish physicians. But the deepest gift of all is that our salvation is of the Jews, through Jesus, the rabbi from Nazareth.

Here is a visual reminder of the truth this sermon tells. Look toward the altar reredos that surrounds the central position of the cross. The twin figures at the top, right and left, are Moses and Isaiah. They were not Americans, Swedes, or Germans. They were Jews. They surround what's front and center on the altar, the empty cross of the risen Lord Jesus Christ.

Through him we are forever bound in a debt of love and gratitude to Israel.

What Manner of Spirit Are We?

March 17, 1963
Luke 9:51-56
F. Dean Lueking, Preacher

When the days drew near for him to be taken up, he set his face to go to Jerusalem. And he sent messengers ahead of him. On their way they entered a village of the Samaritans to make ready for him; but they did not receive him, because his face was set toward Jerusalem. When his disciples James and John saw it, they said, "Lord, do you want us to command fire to come down from heaven and consume them?" But he turned and rebuked them. Then they went on to another village. (Luke 9:51-56)

The Vietnam War of the 1960s tore our nation apart with fiery protests throughout America pitted against passionate justification of its bloody toll. Previously I had not broached the volatile topic from the pulpit. But when the Gospel reading assigned for a Lenten Sunday of that year stated Jesus' rebuke of the disciples' calling down fire on the Samaritans, I could not preach the text as though the Vietnam War was irrelevant. I preached the sermon on March 17, 1963, that appears before you. Rarely have I received a more powerful response at the church door as parishioners lined up to speak their minds. Many expressed affirmation. Some took issue with how I applied the text. But all sensed that silence on the problem was unacceptable.

As a follow up to the sermon, I conferred with the elders and church council about inviting those most directly affected by the issue, young men of draft age, to meet with me in a series of informal meetings to which they and their parents were invited. A dozen or more came. I learned much by listening. My purpose was to offer pastoral support to those who were preparing to join the military as well as to those who chose deferment as conscientious objectors. That meant equipping them with biblical and doctrinal support for faithfulness to the Lord Jesus when tempted to adopt a mindset that sanctioned wanton killing and other sins when far from home and immersed in the macho culture that inevitably seeps into military *service. This sermon was a call to the congregation to face the hard questions of war that were unavoidable. It also deepened my role as the senior pastor into which I would be installed less than a month later.*

A Heritage of Hate

Jesus and his disciples were in unfriendly territory.

They were passing through Samaria on their way to Jerusalem, a region where sharp hostilities between Jews and Samaritans had begun five centuries earlier. When the remnant of exiles returned from Babylon with high hopes of rebuilding the Temple, they sought help from their spiritual kinsmen to the north of Judah. But the Samaritan Jews not only refused help, but they also harassed the returning exiles with military forays as the prophet Ezra tells in his book. Then the Samaritans had a change of heart and offered help. The Judeans scorned it. And thus a long and sad history of hard feelings began. Little wonder, then, that when Jesus led his disciples through Samaria, everybody was on edge.

"Why Not Just Burn Them Up Now?"

As Luke tells the story, Jesus sent a delegation to a certain Samaritan village asking for a hospitable respite as they journeyed southward. The Samaritans' refusal was blunt—neither Jesus nor his disciples could enter for rest and refreshment before moving on. James and John were livid: "Lord, would you not call down fire from heaven and consume them—as Elijah did!" Note how quickly old enmities erupt which lead to this solution: just burn them, level their village, and go on.

Jesus' Disciples Rebuked

Jesus was aghast at the disciples' reaction to being rebuffed. His answer was NO! By no means would he burn the place down, the people with it. He rebukes the disciples sharply, telling them they have no idea what they're asking him to do. He will have none of it. As if what lay before him there was not enough, he had to face it with his heart all the heavier because his own disciples were as hard hearted as the Samaritans who had turned them away.

Jesus, in all his being, could never have participated in blood-letting or anything close to it. "The Son of man came not to destroy men's lives but to save them." It cost him his life on the cross to instill that saving power into the hearts of the disciples, then and now. We, like them, must keep learning the way of grace over and over again. It is in our fallen nature as people born in sin that when we are rebuffed we retaliate in kind—or in worse kind. For being denied hospitality by huffy Samaritans, the disciples proposed a retaliatory strike that would kill every man, woman, and child in the town that rejected them. Think of what it takes to overcome that mindset. No wonder our Lord Jesus had to suffer the unspeakable pain of the cross to do away with our sins that brought him to the cross. Now that he is risen and ruling as our Savior, he's here among us with the good news that his mind becomes our mind as we entrust ourselves to him in faith.

St. Paul says so in one of the most memorable passages of the New Testament:

> Let the same mind be in you that was in Christ Jesus, who, though he was in the form of God, did not regard equality with God as something to be exploited, but emptied himself, taking the form of a slave, being born in human likeness. And being found in human form, he humbled himself and became obedient to the point of death—even death on a cross. Therefore God also highly exalted him and gave him the name that is above every name, so that at the name of Jesus every knee should bend, in heaven and on earth and under the earth, and every tongue should confess that Jesus Christ is Lord, to the glory of God the Father (Phillipians 2:5-11).

I speak his word to you now in the face of the most troubling matter of our day, the war in Vietnam. I do this because today's text demands it. I have not spoken before from the pulpit on this conflict that stirs unrest, protest, and deep division in our land. I preach Christ's truth to you now with fear and trembling, knowing how hard it is to hear but also knowing how strong it is to save us from the sin of silence instead of speech.

Facing Facts

Over the past several years I, like you, have struggled with this mounting conflict in Southeast Asia. Our nation has increased its military presence steadily from the beginning policy of sending advisors. Without question, the embattled people of Vietnam are victims of the mayhem and atrocities of the civil war that has split their nation in two. God alone knows the numbers of innocent people who have perished at the hands of the Vietcong. I have no illusions about the evils of Marxism. Nor do I hold illusions about the corruption of South Vietnam leaders and their readiness to have American soldiers die for their cause.

American bombers raining down incendiary bombs and fiery death on Vietnamese citizens has reached such a stage as to raise actions of protest against our involvement in another nation's internal dispute. During this past year, the number of American boys killed in Vietnam passed 20,000, larger than the total killed during the Korean War. Our military policy calls for the destruction of villages and towns which means civilians, who must find ways of surviving raids that pour down 100,000 tons of napalm.

This is fire from heaven that cannot be blessed in Christ's holy name.

It is wrong. It defies all we hold dear in our faith, and all we stand for as a nation. War in and of itself cannot bring peace. It can only stave off tyranny. War can be justified only as the last resort, only as a defensive action against an assault upon ourselves. As the world's number one military power, we have descended more and more into being the world's policeman. That is a delusion that corrupts us. It's evident from a recent magazine article in which some, not all but some American airmen are heard saying:

> Strafe the town and kill the people, drop napalm in the square,
>
> Get out early every Sunday, catch them at their morning prayer.

Soldiers suffering the futility of the Vietnam War deserve a hearing. Today's *Chicago Tribune* carries the story of a U.S. Marine who wrote home to his little brother one day before he was killed in action: "This war has gone to hell. . . . do anything you can not to get into it.

It's not like the war our Dad fought in. You don't know who or why you're fighting. . . ."

That dead Marine's father added this; "Denny said he and his buddies had reached the point where they wanted to kill anybody they saw. My son's concern stemmed from the fact that our men can't see the enemy. When they see Vietnamese, they don't know if they are friends or enemies. . . ."

I have not been in war. But I respect those who have, especially in Vietnam, who speak from their experience. They deserve to be heard. I speak up for them as one who cares about the increasing number of families whose sons are returning home in body bags.

What Manner of Spirit Are We?

I cannot tell you that your conviction in this agonizing dilemma must be the same as mine. I am not dictating to you, nor am I demanding that at this moment your conscience must inform you exactly as mine informs me. I do say that continued evasive, indecisive, delaying of decision is not to the honor of God's name. Nor does it serve our form of government which can succeed only as we speak with our moral conscience awake and not asleep.

In awareness of our responsibilities as a congregation, I have worked with our parish leaders to set up informal meetings for our young men of draft age and their families. The purpose is to assure them that their congregation cares, listens, and provides a place where they can freely think and speak to each other and, above all, form their decisions on the solid foundation of Scripture as we believe and apply it to this vexing problem. I make this a public invitation here and now. Tell me of your interest. You will receive full information about participating.

Communicate your convictions to your legislators, to our congress, to the president. It is your Christian duty to make your convictions known as servants of the Prince of Peace, our Lord Jesus himself.

It is our duty to care for the refugees of war. Vietnamese who have lost everything need food, clothing, shelter. How can we think of buying another car or adding to our already bulging clothes closet when people for whom God cares and for whom Christ gave himself need help? Our Lutheran Board of World Relief works in tandem with Church World Service to help Vietnamese in their homeland.

We are people of prayer. Not by our wisdom or strength shall peace come, but by God's doing. Keep praying, "Thy will be done on earth as it is in heaven"—and think of what this petition means now. And take to heart the Lord's solemn warning that all who take the sword shall perish by the sword (Matthew 26:20). God have mercy upon us. God grant us the mind of Christ Jesus! Amen.

How Far Will God Go?

August 1964
Matthew 21: 33-43
F. Dean Lueking, *Preacher*

"Listen to another parable. There was a landowner who planted a vineyard, put a fence around it, dug a wine press in it, and built a watchtower. Then he leased it to tenants and went to another country. When the harvest time had come, he sent his slaves to the tenants to collect his produce. But the tenants seized his slaves and beat one, killed another, and stoned another. Again he sent other slaves, more than the first; and they treated them in the same way. Finally he sent his son to them, saying, 'They will respect my son.' But when the tenants saw the son, they said to themselves, 'This is the heir; come, let us kill him and get his inheritance.' So they seized him, threw him out of the vineyard, and killed him. Now when the owner of the vineyard comes, what will he do to those tenants?" They said to him, "He will put those wretches to a miserable death, and lease the vineyard to other tenants who will give him the produce at the harvest time."

Jesus said to them, "Have you never read in the scriptures:
    'The stone that the builders rejected
        has become the cornerstone;[a]
    this was the Lord's doing,
        and it is amazing in our eyes'?
Therefore I tell you, the kingdom of God will be taken away from you and given to a people that produces the fruits of the kingdom." (Matthew 21:33-43)

No event in my first year as senior pastor of Grace Lutheran Church was more memorable for me than participating in the March on Washington on August 28, 1963. I joined with over 250,000 other Americans who filled to overflowing the Mall of the Washington Monument to hear Martin Luther King, Jr. deliver his "I

Have A Dream" speech. I will never forget the thrill of goose bumps running up and down my spine when hearing King's soaring voice, in rising cadences, come to those closing words from an old spiritual: "Free at last, free at last, thank God almighty, we are free at last."

Upon returning home, I had to keep three things in mind when thinking about how to communicate my March on Washington experience. First, we at Grace were an all-white congregation in a nearly all-white community composed of people with a wide spectrum of views on racial integration in general and the role of Martin Luther King in particular. Second, only four months had passed since I had been installed as the senior pastor at Grace, even though I had eight years of assistant pastor experience behind me in serving the congregation. Third, 1963 had been dubbed "a long hot summer" of increasing racial unrest across the land which raised tensions that our members felt along with countless others.

Mentioning the March in sermons from the pulpit did not strike me as a good idea for several reasons. The point was not to showcase my going to Washington, nor were my feelings about it the main thing. Moreover, the pulpit is limited to one-way communication. And while an open forum setting would be necessary for an open exchange of views, what usually happens is that the more vocal speak up and the less so say nothing or stay away altogether.

A clue to a better idea lay in the advice I had received from the elders with whom I had conferred prior to going to Washington. These three experienced men of faith were elders in the true sense of the term, people I greatly respected for their seasoned faith and proven commitments. They heard me out when I informed them why I thought I should join the March as an act of faith. Their response was brief and to the point: "Pastor, do what your conscience tells you to do. And when you return, remember that we who stayed home didn't experience it first hand as you did."

While mulling over that sound advice, I hit upon an idea that did not make me and my Washington experience the center piece but offered a practical way for Grace members who were ready for it to take part in inter-racial Bible study groups with Negro Lutherans (Negro was 1963 speak) that enabled friendships to form, differing backgrounds shared, racial issues addressed with more realism, and biases overcome by listening and talking together. I sought the help of three pastors serving black Lutheran congregations in Chicago in finding black Lutherans interested *in meeting with white Lutherans. By late 1963, monthly Bible study groups were underway with around sixty people taking part. Interest spread as word got around. There was some pushback from a handful of Grace members who were not ready, but no major upheaval in the congregation occurred since it was voluntary and scripturally based.*

About a year after these inter-racial exchanges of faith and friendship were well started, I felt the time was right to mention my participation in the Washington experience and the inter-racial Bible study groups formed as a consequence. I did so, making it more of an invitation to join in the benefits of what was going on, rather than a report on my spending a memorable day in Washington D.C. a year earlier.

Here is the sermon from August 1964, preached on Jesus' Parable of the Wicked Vinedressers.

Thoughtful readers of the Bible have noted this about Jesus' parables: Whenever the parable features images drawn from nature, an air of peace and serenity dominates. Think, for example, of his parables of the mustard seed, a flock of sheep, or the lilies of the field which describe the kingdom of God in action. But whenever man enters the story another mood sets in—disobedience and violence as signs of human sin which infects everything. Examples: the parables of the Prodigal Son, the Dishonest Steward, and especially today's parable of the Wicked Vinedressers found in Matthew 21.

The story tells of human nature at its worst. These thuggish hired hands, called Wicked Vinedressers in Jesus' story, show how deeply evil is lodged in the human heart. That sinfulness attacks God's kingly rule with pitiless violence, as those who are supposed to be caretakers of the vineyard work systematic mayhem against those sent to harvest the grapes. Finally they plot and carry out the murder of the landowner's son who is the heir, to whom the vineyard belongs. Yet, back to back with that harsh teaching within the parable, there is also word of the Lord's boundless patience and love in promising new servants through whom the vineyard has a future. That is the note of surprising grace that overcomes the hopelessness of the human condition without it.

The first great truth here is heartening. Jesus tells of the length to which God's patience reaches as he bears with us and with our world. Who of us, if we were the landowners, would treat the rebellious tenants like God treats them? Who of us would send one, two, then three servants as messengers and then, when they are stoned and killed, send more reserves to make things right? And supremely, who of us would finally send our only son to be rejected and killed by such a gang of rowdies?

Just think: how deep is the truth offered us today! Stand back from this story and imagine the length the Lord's mercy reaches. How patient, how forbearing he is with us! Jesus asks us in all earnestness to see ourselves in the long history of His saving care for the world. God sent many a messenger to Israel of old, and not one of them won a popularity contest. Yes, they comforted the afflicted; they also afflicted the comfortable. The prophets of the Old Testament did root up and tear down the prideful arrogance when it showed itself in the rebellion of God's people against their calling. But instead of sending a thunderbolt down to destroy them, God's patient admonishing, forbearing, appeal continued on for centuries.

The prophet Jeremiah is an example. He lived in times much like our own, when people sought power in order to control and dominate. Jeremiah lived out his prophetic calling right in the thick of it, exhorting Israel not to put their trust in Egypt or any world power, nor in chariots and horses. Trust God above all things and follow him! For this truth-telling, Jeremiah was put in chains, jailed numerous times, thrown into a dungeon, and carried off captive to Egypt. In all of this he was a messenger of God's patience that outlasted God's wrath and judgment. This is the first truth Jesus teaches in this parable.

There's another truth that comes through clearly. It is about human nature, our human nature. Why is it that people who are hired hands get the notion they own everything? That everything has somehow become theirs? Here's the truth for us to grasp: whenever we, in whatever form, go from being servants to owners, we're in trouble. God gives us this vast, wonderful world on loan. We're created to care for it as faithful stewards—not just in regard to our daily necessities, food and shelter, but also our capacities of mind and energies for work.

These are ours by loan. We are responsible for giving an account of our stewardship. How clear is it that when we've worked hard for what we possess, we're told that we are caretakers, not owners. How quickly does "that's mine!" take over? Are you like me, finding it so hard to own, the truth this parable tells us that each of us, in some way or another, is in on some form of embezzlement of all the gifts that God loans out to us? That we confuse our status as stewards with the assumption we're owners?

Now we must face together the challenge of applying this parable to a fact of our time. The fact is racial prejudice and its bitter fruit. The challenge is to live the Gospel of Christ's reconciling grace in a way that overcomes racial injustice and moves toward integration. It is important to see the distinction between racial desegregation and racial integration. Desegregation is a matter of civil law and legislation. It comes via pressure and enforcement, whether we like it or not. That's how it is. The world of which we are a part lives under civil law; we as Lutherans ought to understand that as part of God's ruling via his "left hand"—i.e., his Law and the institutions of state which embody it. This belongs in our land; it is written into our nation's constitution which we respect.

But desegregation is not integration. Integration can't be enforced by civil law. There is one power the church knows that creates the inner attitude and will to be my brother's keeper. That is the fruit of the Gospel, the good news that God loves the world and gave his Son over to death on a cross in our behalf. Jesus took upon himself the full weight of the sins of the world, including the sins of racial bias, and suffered its punishment that was ours by right. God is the Landowner who has not left the vineyard to its own destruction, but raised up Jesus to do for us what we cannot do for ourselves—reconcile us to God as his forgiven children. In bringing us back to God's family, Jesus makes us brothers and sisters. No color barrier can block that belonging. This is God's "right hand" work, making us right with him by faith so that we can now belong to each other in love.

I realize that the present racial strife that dominates the news is disturbing. The temptation is to blame others, particularly those whose skin is black and who are now speaking up about what they endure as heirs of slaves. We must face that history and do our best to see its cruelty by putting ourselves into the shoes of those who bear its burden.

In August 1963 I heard Martin Luther King, Jr., appeal to all Americans to come to Washington to show support for changing the long-term effects of the curse of racial injustice. I went. I did so because it was in my conscience to participate in the March on Washington. I heard Dr. King speak powerfully of the dream of a racially divided America taking bold steps to come together across that deep divide. The speech thrilled me. In returning from that experience, I have valued the advice of our Grace elders with whom I conferred before I went—to follow what my conscience told me to do and to remember that you of the Grace congregation did not experience that March as I did. Nor are all of you of the same mind regarding the leadership of Martin Luther King. I have not forced my impressions upon you, nor have I even spoken of it from the pulpit since I returned. I do not think that this is a best setting for getting at what needs getting at in this explosive issue.

And so I have tried to translate my experience in the March on Washington into something you can experience. The inter-racial Bible study groups that have been put together in the past year involves some of our Grace members with black Lutherans from First Immanuel, First St. Paul, and Ebenezer congregations in Chicago. About sixty or so people are taking part, meeting once a month in each other's homes in each other's respective neighborhoods. The content of the sessions is drawn from Scripture, specifically the New Testament Epistle of Colossians. It's so important to meet other Lutherans of another color first as fellow believers, then as friends with names, faces, and experiences, and learn and grow with them as we do what the church is called to do—be a leaven, a light, and a guide through turbulent times.

I invite you to join in what's going on. No one is forced. Joining in may not be your choice. But please do not think or speak ill of this effort. That would be slandering an action based on mutual study of God's Word. Do not misrepresent this modest effort as something the church has no business doing.

I am also aware that our inter-congregation effort is but a drop in the bucket when placed against all that's happening in our city and land. But it is no less than that. It counts for far more than it looks like, in that it is done in the Lord's name and for His sake. This is doing our part as farm hands in the vineyard of God the Landowner. The key to it is faith active in love. We are to plant the seeds of healing, helping and living out the faith once delivered to the saints, for which many have suffered and died before we came along.

Must our Lord always go to the Calvary of the world's sins alone? Is there no one willing to bear the burden His cross lays upon those who claim His name and call ourselves Christians? Luther once said that the Gospel is like a thunder shower that comes along, refreshes, and moves to another place. The opportunity to respond to the Gospel comes. And it goes. We can meet it. Or we can miss it. To be sure, this sermon stresses the patience of God. But that must not detract from the urgency of the now, of this moment, of this opportune season, to be under God's service and active in His mission as His kingly rule moves from place to place. And God plays no favorites. He will put others in our place if we are deaf to His call and turn down his appeal to us as workers in His Vineyard. That's clear from the text we hear today.

Dear people of God, open your hearts to Christ's love. And open your minds to how you can serve as a reconciler in a racially biased community. When heart and mind are united in love upward to God and outward to those close by, God's will is done on earth as it is in heaven. For that we pray. To that we commit ourselves, not as those who test God's patience, but those who show the signs of it working where it is sorely needed.

The Call Is Severe, the Caller Merciful
The Ordination of Mr. Peter Marty into the Office of the Holy Ministry

September 7, 1986
Luke 14:25-33
F. Dean Lueking, Preacher

Now large crowds were traveling with him; and he turned and said to them, "Whoever comes to me and does not hate father and mother, wife and children, brothers and sisters, yes, and even life itself, cannot be my disciple. Whoever does not carry the cross and follow me cannot be my disciple. For which of you, intending to build a tower, does not first sit down and estimate the cost, to see whether he has enough to complete it? Otherwise, when he has laid a foundation and is not able to finish, all who see it will begin to ridicule him, saying, 'This fellow began to build and was not able to finish.' Or what king, going out to wage war against another king, will not sit down first and consider whether he is able with ten thousand to oppose the one who comes against him with twenty thousand? If he cannot, then, while the other is still far away, he sends a delegation and asks for the terms of peace. So therefore, none of you can become my disciple if you do not give up all your possessions."
(Luke 14:25-33)

In 1948, the then Grace pastor, Otto Geiseman, set in place a policy of calling and ordaining Concordia Seminary graduates for a two-year period as assistant pastors in the congregation. The purpose was to ground them in congregation-based ministry and encourage their part-time graduate study in the Chicago area. The goal was to increase the skills requisite for excellence as ministers of the Gospel.

I preached this sermon on the occasion of the ordination of Peter Marty into the Office of the Ministry. He was the fifteenth in the series of assistant pastors who preceded him from 1948 on. He arrived at Grace with a richly diverse background—study at Yale Divinity School, a volunteer for a year in Cameroon in West Africa, and as the third son in the household of Martin and Elsa Marty. After his two years at Grace from 1986-1988 he went on to a congregation in the Kansas City area and after that became the senior pastor St. Paul's Lutheran Church, Davenport, Iowa, a flagship congregation of over 3,000 in the ELCA. Along the way he has become widely appreciated as a columnist in The Lutheran magazine and in 2016 became the publisher of the Christian Century magazine, America's foremost Protestant magazine.

Geiseman's concept of a two-year term call was unique and controversial when it began in the late 1940s. A view widespread in the LCMS tradition held that a term call for a specific time period was an affront to the work of the Holy Spirit in determining when a pastor should enter and leave a call to serve a congregation. Geiseman thought otherwise. He saw it as an act of serving the Holy Spirit's work of equipping and calling men (only men, at that time at Grace) to the pastorate and mentoring them toward continued learning while practicing parish ministry as well as furthering their ministry skills through continuing education at the graduate level. He had earned a doctorate in pastoral ethics at a nearby Lutheran seminary throughout the challenging years of building and paying for the new Grace Church during the late 1930s and '40s. In passing that experience on, he handed down a legacy of combining pastoral ministry with continued learning for the sake of being at one's best for the high calling of being "just a parish pastor." It is a model that merits attention today as the demands of pastoral ministry grow more complex as well as more satisfying.

During my years as senior pastor from 1963 to 1998, fourteen assistants were called and ordained for a period of two years—some for three—and then moved on. All engaged in some form of graduate education; each contributed uniquely to the enrichment of the overall ministry at Grace. (My own doctorate in church history at the University of Chicago during my assistant pastoral years was intended to prepare me for return to Japan for a missionary vocation where I had vicared from 1951 to '53; that was changed by Geiseman's illness and death in 1962.) Grace congregation and school have been greatly enriched by these assistant pastors who have shared in all aspects of the ministry at Grace. Also, throughout nearly five decades, the pastors and people of Grace maintained a close tie with the administration and faculty of a major seminary, a bond that deserves renewing and imaginative reapplication in this day of change and challenge in what it means to prepare people for the front line of the church in the world—the local congregation.

The program ended after Concordia Seminary became Concordia Seminary in Exile and ultimately merged with three other ELCA seminaries. In 1990 Rev. Leon Rosenthal was called as an associate pastor, beginning a new tradition of associate pastors which continues to this day.

Today we gather from far and near to participate in the ordination of Peter Marty into the pastoral ministry. Here he is before us—hopeful and excited to think about what this day begins, as we share in that same excitement and hope.

The text for today's sermon, however, is not one I have chosen. It has chosen me. It is the Gospel reading from Luke 14 appointed for this Sunday. Its tone is sober. Its content jarring—so much so we must listen up and prepare for a shock: "If anyone comes to me and does not hate his own father and mother, wife and children, and brothers and sisters, yes, and even his own life, he cannot be my disciple."

This text for *this* day? Peter, can it be that Jesus means you when he calls you to hate your father and mother, your wife and such children as shall be given you, and even your own life? Here sits Susan beside you. Your father nearby. And all of us who are here with love and high hopes for you—are you to *hate* the whole job lot of us?

The text is what it is—one of the hard sayings of Jesus that is not to be toned down but lifted up. Hating all that would slip in to replace the living, risen Lord as first in the heart is the strongest possible verb for the strongest possible calamity for you and the ministry into which you enter today. It belongs with other sayings of Jesus that push language to its limits in order to make the truth overwhelmingly clear, such as ". . . easier for a camel to pass through the eye of a needle than for a rich man to enter the kingdom of heaven," Jesus said. "If anyone strikes you on the cheek, turn to him the other one," Jesus said. To the disciples who begged Jesus to call down fire from heaven upon the stubborn Samaritans, Jesus said, "You don't know what manner of spirit you are!" When his mother and brothers warned him to stay out of Jerusalem and come home to the safety of Nazareth, Jesus looked at those around him and said, "Here are my mother, my brothers and my sisters." To the devil who tempted him to put bread, spectacle, and the earthly realms ahead of his Father in heaven Jesus said a three-fold No.

Jesus means the severity of his word to you today, Peter, because the temptation you face is real. It is to domesticate, compromise, bend, and reshape Jesus down to what works, what pleases, what makes common sense in a religion reduced to what's reasonable. That temptation hits hardest when it comes in the form of putting the one dearest to you, the one closest in family or friendship, into the place which belongs to the Lord alone. That happens, even in our own souls, because we are all partners in a fallen humanity. We do not love, trust, and fear God first in the heart. Is there need to go on at length about the evidence all around?

Let one man tell us this truth in his own way. Garrison Keillor's *Lake Woebegon Days* tells of a returnee to his mythical hometown from sophisticated Boston. His life, he admits, has been an unending rebellion against his parents and everything about his Lake Woebegon beginnings:

> I wanted some good years thinking proudly that I wasn't anything like you. Having grown up with ugly wallpaper, I painted my walls off-white and thought I'd finally arrived. Bought a white couch, yours having been purple. My life looks like February.

A great deal of life around us in 1986 looks like February because sin is sin and the consequences are like a permanent February with no hint of spring ahead nor any trace of an autumn beauty to cherish in grateful remembering.

The fix that leaves you in, and all of us with you, is this: we cannot of our own reason or strength believe in Jesus Christ our Lord, come to him, love him first the heart, or enter the high calling of pastor as though we've got it all together. We cannot. Absolutely not. The Caller is severe because he knows that gap between what we've got and what he needs is unbridgeable.

The Caller is merciful beyond all that you—or we with you—could desire or deserve. Mercy is God's full-to-overflowing loving kindness and forgiving mercy that took Jesus his Son to the cross, to accomplish there what we could not accomplish for ourselves.

His mercy is upon you, Peter, and has been from the day of your baptism onward.

You have come to embrace and own that mercy by the power of God's own indwelling Holy Spirit. Among the countless events in your life that confirm that mercy, I mention this one. When you were an ocean and a continent away from home several years ago, devoting fourteen months of missionary service in Cameroon, you were handed a telegram one day that you dreaded to open but knew it was coming. It told of your mother's death after her good fight of faith against cancer. So far from home and family, so far from Elsa who bore you into the world, you were nonetheless given grace—through your tears and heartache—to commend her to God. Your mother is at rest in Christ's peace today. That is no small part of the peace that keeps you on this wonderfully meaningful day as well.

Christ the Lord did not, has not, will not fail you. Ahead lie moments of joy and fulfillment that will make you a Hallelujah from head to foot. Ahead of you are moments that will bring you to your knees in humility and bewilderment. You've been promised that that nothing can separate you from the love of God—but not promised that there won't be plenty that will try.

As you work your way into serving God's people at Grace, you'll find that they will keep on teaching you a great deal about the severity of Christ's call and the merciful Caller that he is. Seminary and university classroom was one form of education for ministry—and an enormously important and richly blessed one as well. A salute to all those teachers today! Here—all around and behind you in the church today are new teachers who have much to give. Day by day the baptized people of God who are his ministers in the daily life of the world go out to serve and return here for refreshment and the Bread of Life in the Gospel you preach and teach and the sacraments you administer. People will astound you, confound you, bless you, test you, and ultimately pray for you and minister to you in ways that will make your heart glad. Welcome to the ministry given all of us, and to you as Pastor Marty in our midst.

Grace people, welcome Peter and Susan with the fullness of grace that makes Grace Church a place of blessing, creative faithfulness, and adventuresome discipleship. Those of you who bring us the great music of our heritage, thank you for the inspiration that you will bring Peter and all of us with him! Those of you who teach children in our school—with whom Peter will join as one who loves kids and helps them grow in faith, hope, and love—welcome a partner in the work! Leaders in the many aspects of our congregation's life, we have a gifted, caring, good-humored young man to help you be at your best for your work.

In the Ordination Rite today we hear these words. I quote them now, Peter, as a word of special power and blessing as you begin a ministry that—God willing—will have a very long, wide, and deep reach into the decades ahead:

> Care for God's people. Bear their burdens. Do not betray their confidence. So discipline yourself in life and teaching that you preserve the truth, giving no occasion for false security or illusory hope. Witness faithfully in word and deed to everyone. Give and receive comfort as you serve within the church and take your place in the community beyond. And be of good courage, for God has called you, and your labor in the Lord is not in vain.

Impoverished By Wealth

October 15, 1995
Luke 16:19-31
F. Dean Lueking, Preacher

"There was a rich man who was dressed in purple and fine linen and who feasted sumptuously every day. And at his gate lay a poor man named Lazarus, covered with sores, who longed to satisfy his hunger with what fell from the rich man's table; even the dogs would come and lick his sores. The poor man died and was carried away by the angels to be with Abraham. The rich man also died and was buried. In Hades, where he was being tormented, he looked up and saw Abraham far away with Lazarus by his side. He called out, 'Father Abraham, have mercy on me, and send Lazarus to dip the tip of his finger in water and cool my tongue; for I am in agony in these flames.' But Abraham said, 'Child, remember that during your lifetime you received your good things, and Lazarus in like manner evil things; but now he is comforted here, and you are in agony. Besides all this, between you and us a great chasm has been fixed, so that those who might want to pass from here to you cannot do so, and no one can cross from there to us.' He said, 'Then, father, I beg you to send him to my father's house—for I have five brothers—that he may warn them, so that they will not also come into this place of torment.' Abraham replied, 'They have Moses and the prophets; they should listen to them.' He said, 'No, father Abraham; but if someone goes to them from the dead, they will repent.' He said to him, 'If they do not listen to Moses and the prophets, neither will they be convinced even if someone rises from the dead.'"
(Luke 16:19-31)

Grace Church members are, *comparatively speaking, well off materially as well as spiritually. Most of us live in homes that are well kept, comfortable, and on their way to being paid for. We are middle and upper middle class folks, with a few below that line and an opposite few well over it. Aware of our economic profile, I often stressed fruitfulness in stewardship of our gifts and generosity sharing them. I do not recall urging the biblical tithe, but I wish I had. It is a well-established discipline in Scripture. In our household, we practice it. But for whatever reason, I did not touch upon it very often. In the sermon cited here, however, I did apply Jesus' Parable of the Rich Man and Lazarus to the peril of idolizing wealth. Thus the title, "Impoverished by Wealth," centered on this problem: the rich man in the parable never saw the impoverished Lazarus at his door day in and day out. His material wealth blinded him to the true treasure of the heart which is Jesus himself. As the parable tells, when death claimed both men, their destinies were exactly reversed. The rich man, suffering hell's miseries, lost his chance not only for his own rescue but also that of his family left behind. It is here and now that the warning comes to avoid the blight of serving Mammon first in life. Today comes the call to be stewards of God's bounty, not sacrificing it to the false god of being obsessed by always wanting more.*

This parable of Jesus is not about either the furniture of heaven or the temperature of hell. It is about "hearing Moses and the prophets" and the whole truth of God. Today. Here. Now.

We must hear it as a people in danger. What danger? Violence in the streets? Drugs that destroy? Lust, gluttony, anger out of control? Of course. But not primarily these.

The danger we're in comes from idolizing wealth. An idol, as Luther reminds us, is that to which we look for all security and good. When that's first in the heart, we're living under threat. It's an insidious threat, creeping up from the inside without obvious signs or siren warnings. It's being poor in soul because making money becomes an end in itself instead of a means for which God intended.

We Are the World's One-Fifth

Let's look at facts about where we Americans stand in the world's human family. Day by day we spend $99,000,000 on lottery tickets and $52,435 on national debt reduction (from The Index, *Harper's* magazine, November 1994 issue). Why this binge, this national mania? It's a clear sign of how we're impoverishing ourselves as a nation through an addictive notion that a one dollar ticket will pay off in a multi-million win. I read the recent news article on the Chicago woman who put four quarters into a Las Vegas slot machine and staggered off with 1.3 million—to be met at O'Hare by reporters as an instant millionaire. Does anyone see the dark side, how the bonanza is the beginning of a nightmare? On and on I can go with such illustrations from daily life.

But I won't. I know how hard it is to convince you—or myself—that you and I are rich people. It is so hard to see ourselves, as over one half of the world's population struggle on $400 a year or less. Think of the things that have become common place in our lives in our part of the world over the past fifty years: television, polio vaccine, frozen foods, fast foods, Xerox, contact lenses, the pill, credit cards, dish washers, electric blankets, air conditioners, computers, jet travel, voice mail, etc.

Over half of the people in the world do not have these things. In fact, they can hardly dream of having them. We do. Who, then, are the well off? We are. You and I.

The Fateful Reversal

These facts are laid out in some detail to get your attention and bring you back to Jesus' parable with its stern truth about how the sin of avarice brings on impoverishment of life. The rich man in Jesus' story suffered torment. Poor Lazarus, the beggar at the rich man's door day in and day out, is brought by the angels to Abraham's bosom. What brought the rich man down and poor Lazarus up was neither wealth nor poverty, but the rich man's blindness to God the giver. He had all good things in his affluent life, but not the eyes to see his brother Lazarus outside his door, hungry and in rags.

How can that blindness afflict your "eyes of the heart" as St. Paul speaks of the soul's vision? To what are you blind? As I name two such things I ask you to take them to heart carefully.

Self-sufficiency is the first. It turns up in phrases like this: "I've worked hard for what I've got. . . . I've accomplished plenty. . . . I deserve what I've earned. . . . I've climbed the ladder on my own." With that mindset comes the idea that human ingenuity, human muscle, human accomplishment begins and ends with us. Frank Leahy, former coach at Notre Dame, was asked whether the prayers of the nuns on campus made any difference in the game scores. "Yes, when my players are bigger than the other side," was his answer. It reveals the old problem. My muscle, my players, my skill, my game. Maybe in football. But not in life under God. Self-sufficiency is not the mark of life under God. Self is everything.

Self-indulgence is another impoverishment that comes from idolizing wealth. The rich man feasted sumptuously, dressed like one right out of Barney's of New York. But the rich man could not for a moment imagine what the forces were that brought Lazarus to his plight. He was blinded by self-indulgence. That rules out any grasp of what poverty is. Addiction to wealth enlarges the appetite for more wealth. It feeds on self-absorption, which in turn leads to misery. There is a great deceit buried in self-indulgence.

Enriched by His Poverty

Enough diagnosing the malady of wealth's impoverishing force. You get it, I trust. Now let's turn to the remedy.

People of faith: our Lord Jesus Christ became poor for our sakes, so that in his poverty we might have the wealth that does not impoverish but lasts. It is this treasure: he who knew no sin gave himself upon the cross to forgive our sin. His grace is the true treasure of the heart. It cannot rust away, nor can any moth destroy it.

Jesus gave himself unconditionally, in sacrificial love and forgiving mercy. It cost him his life. All this—for you, for me, for all of us! His Spirit opens blind eyes to see what true wealth is, how it can be shared, how it establishes wisdom in handling our possessions and generosity in enriching others by welcoming each other.

This is a great miracle. I am increasingly convinced that people who know God's giving and give accordingly are walking sermons. I think of a businessman I once visited at his luxurious office. I began talking to him about giving. He responded to that visit and that conversation with a long litany of his business woes and the besetting problems of unstable economies. I left that visit wondering if he could understand his impoverishment. Of course, we always have the Rush

Limbaughs to set things straight, to explain that the Lazarus of Jesus' story is really a lush, a welfare barnacle on the body politic, who deserves the rags he's wearing and the sores on his body. But that affluent businessman I mentioned has had a change in his life and fortunes. I did not cite him as a straw man, but a human being capable of repentance and change. That's the great turn in his life that has put him on a path that enriches in faith, hope, and love. He's listening to what his wealth is for. God-willing, he will come through to a new maturity about himself and what the Holy Spirit is accomplishing in him and through him. I'm learning, too.

Sometimes it is tragedy that makes us see our impoverishment and open our eyes to God's riches. I have a pastoral friend who serves in the South. He lost his young daughter to leukemia and fought off bitterness and rage for a time. Then he came to see it all in a new light. He writes, "When I began to ask, not why she died but why she was even born, why she was born to us as long as we had her, why her beauty and love blessed us . . . then I began to view her—and all of life—as a gift. I could use the time of her being with us as a time of thanksgiving that she had been given to us at all." Do you see a great wealth here? One far greater than all else in life, and greater than death itself? Own that wealth in your soul, mind, and life. Let God be God at all times and places, and especially when your impoverishment and helplessness are most painfully real.

Howard Thurman, the late, great, black American Christian leader, knew poverty in his life. Hear his words: "When we have exhausted our store of endurance, when our strength has failed ere the day is half done, when we reach the end of our hoarded resources, our Father's full giving is only begun."

People of Grace, we are rich on a world scale, but that can vanish in a day, an hour, an instant. Count your true wealth as the grace of Jesus Christ at work in you—and that includes your pocketbook and bank account. Share it generously. Be disciplined in your stewardship. All this is meant for today. For here and now.

I am not called to serve your procrastinating. I am not authorized to tell you there will always be a tomorrow or some later time. God comes first in the heart—now. Always now.

Justice, Kindness, Humility

January 31, 1993
Micah 6:8
F. Dean Lueking, Preacher

And what does the Lord require of you but to do justice, love mercy, and walk humbly with your God. (Micah 6:8)

Early in 1990 a phone call came from a local organization serving homeless people. The caller asked whether Grace Church might take a turn with neighboring congregations as a one-night-a-week shelter for homeless people. I responded by saying that the process of approval would involve both the leadership of the congregation as well as that of the town, and that it would probably take about a year to gain both. The estimate turned out to be accurate.

I began by laying out the challenge to our elders. They listened, asked good questions, and concurred that we should participate. The Church Council also concurred after several meetings for the purpose of further inquiry. I thought that it would be appropriate as a next step to get the River Forest Town Board to hear us out and see where matters stood. Several open meetings followed. The expected objections came as no surprise since the idea was well covered in the town newspaper. That publicity raised concerns among those who were worried about the effects of our mission on their property values. In thinking back on it, I now realize we should have done a more thorough job of explaining our own measures of insuring safety and heading off stereotypes of homeless fellow citizens. What came as a welcome surprise, however, were the comments of River Forest residents who not only supported the plan but sent contributions to the church to help cover costs.

What resolved the matter in our behalf was a timely comment made by Grace member and attorney, Dick Martens, in one of the many public hearings held in the River Forest Village Hall. He reminded everyone that the First Amendment of the United States Constitution states that church and state are separated so that the state cannot prevent the free exercise of religion (in our view, housing the homeless being such) nor can the church establish itself as the religion of the state. The approval of the River Forest Town Board took the form of a no objection statement.

The congregation's approval to participate required several open meetings to learn how the plan would work as well as to receive pro and con response. In my memory there were several parishioners who spoke strongly against our participation, repeating negative views expressed earlier by neighbors who spoke in opposition. To my regret, these members left the congregation when the outcome was a strong majority vote in favor of participating. When a Chicago Tribune reporter covering that final meeting asked a Grace member for comment, Adrian Rott answered in a sentence that summed it up well: "Fear and love met today, and love prevailed."

During the several years of our participation, an average of twenty to thirty guests were hosted in the Grace gym. They were mostly single men, but some couples with young children occasionally were present. A hot supper was prepared and served by a team of volunteers. Several Grace men were present throughout the night to see that all went well. Another volunteer group served breakfast. The guests were on their way by 7:00 a.m. Grace member Mark Lucht was a symbol of the larger number of parishioners who made the plan work well in the early 1990s. Our participation ended after two years. The reason was the awareness that more than emergency shelter was required to meet the broader set of needs that people in such circumstances have. As true as that was, in my view we stopped too soon. Plans to resolve the deeper needs never materialized.

On January 31, 1993, I preached this sermon on the Micah 6:8 text, the assigned Old Testament lesson for the day and one of the great biblical texts that speak to the controversial action of serving homeless people. The sermon begins by acknowledging our struggle, then goes on to let the forceful appeal of the text speak for itself. The sermon was consequential for our acceptance of our place in this form of mission to the wider community that was new to us at Grace Church.

We are a congregation in controversy. It arises inevitably out of our current struggle on how best to obey God's call to minister to homeless people here in our community by providing a Saturday night shelter in our gym for people with no place to go. I use my words carefully here. The issue cannot be whether we care for them. God's word is clear: we must. The issue is how we care. Some say—direct the homeless to existing shelters in Chicago. Others say: open our own doors and do our part here and now.

Interestingly, and with direct relevance to what we face, the Old Testament lesson for today tells of another controversy—the one that God has with his chosen people. As the prophet Micah sets the scene in the southern Kingdom of Judah seven centuries before Christ, God himself holds court. He calls witnesses from all creation. He calls his people to account for their sins of greed, exploiting power, commercial fraud, and especially for the sin of trying to buy off God's wrathful judgment through the exercise of religious ritual.

As the gap widened between the haves and have-nots, God pleads for true piety that connects altar and market place, Scripture and just government, prayer and caring for the poor. I did not choose this text for this Sunday; it was chosen for me by the lectionary. It reads as follows: "He has told you, O mortal, what is good; and what does the Lord require of you but to do justice, love mercy, and walk humbly with your God" (Micah 6:8).

On the surface our current controversy appears to be one of our own doing. But the Micah 6 text takes us deeper. It is God who is calling us to account. He is stirring the pot of controversy. He is putting us face to face with a dilemma few of us can grasp: to live this day with no place to spend this night. Our winter of discontent is a clash of priorities and commitments, his and ours. Until we see this clearly, we miss both the diagnosis and the remedy of our dilemma.

An amazing, truly unprecedented concentration of fear, gossip, accusation, as well as faith and faith intentions have been mixed together here in recent months. While we all can be penitent over our own sins, we should not drown in guilt over where we are. Sometimes the Lord leads us gently; at other times he prods us in the ribs till we notice. The latter describes best what is going on currently. The Lord we love and serve has a purpose in all this that we wish would just go away. It won't.

We have a resolution to our controversy that is set before us. It is one we not have chosen. Keeping in mind the courtroom setting of Micah (6:1-7), another enters the scene. It is the Messiah foretold by Micah in the preceding chapter (5:2-5). The promise is that a Savior shall be born in the Judean town of Bethlehem, One who shall stand and feed his flock in the strength of the Lord and bring peace to the ends of the earth.

Jesus is that messianic Lord who has come, the One through whom all things were created. Yet as he humbled himself to enter into our human form, he had no place to lay his head. Jesus was homeless. Our Lord, who saved us from sin and death, had no roof over his head he could call his own. Let that sink in, really take hold. How often do we remember that Jesus never owned a foot of real estate, so that in every homeless man or woman or child we serve today means serving our Savior himself! Jesus has slept all through the cold winter's night in the front seat of a car parked in our church lot.

Do we serve him or pass him on to someplace else?

> "Inasmuch as you have done it to the least of these my brothers and sisters, you have done it to me."
> (Matthew 25:40)

In raising the crucified Christ from the dead, God reclaims lost lives at every level, from the homeless poor to the mansion rich. Coming to us with undeserved mercy and the forgiveness of our sins, he makes his home in every heart opened to him. As Christ dwells within you and me, we grow into a mind like his. We gain the will to do what is required of us, to do justice and love mercy and walk humbly with him. Notice that the conjunction is "and," not "or." Thus it is not that we do justice but not love mercy, or that we love mercy but do not walk humbly with our God. It's "and," not "or."

The New Testament Scriptures confirm the Old Testament mandate: "Is not this the fast that I choose: to loose the bonds of injustice, to undo the thongs of the yoke, to let the oppressed go free, and to break every yoke? Is it not to share your bread with the hungry, and bring the homeless poor into your house; when you see the naked to cover them, and not hide yourself from your own kin" (Isaiah 58:6-8).

We must deal with fears, those coming from our fellow towns people who place property value over human value. We must deal with the fears coming—I am grieved to say—from some within our congregation who suffer from the same blighted view of all that the mission of the Gospel includes. In recent weeks those fears have taken unprecedented form, placing hundreds of sheets of slander in mail boxes, playing on every fear except the fear of God, distorting our mission, harassing our leaders, and tempting us to trade our Gospel heritage for a mess of pottage.

Grace members: we will not be bullied. No wearing down, now. Would God call us to care for the least and then not equip us to carry out our mission? Would he give us his command without supplying the spiritual stamina to live it out?

"Do justice," he calls out to every one of us. Homelessness cannot be dismissed as the plight of those who deserve it by their own sloth and stupidity. It comes about through a myriad of gnarled problems of the haves having more and the have-nots having ever less. That's been the bane of American society that hides an ominous truth underneath our prosperity. If you're not of the right skin color, the right ethnic background, the right access to privilege, you don't get in on the abundant life. That's the illusion we must defy.

Thus homelessness as the prime mark of poverty begins with greed, injustice, and all-around sin at every level. Justice counts tremendously in making the law prevent grievous economic and social inequality that is brought on by scorn for the poor. There are hopeful signs, however. Last month the Zoning Board of River Forest reversed a ban on a house of worship used to exercise its religious mission under the First Amendment. Now it is our turn to stand and deliver. We are asked to be a Saturday night shelter in our building. Six other congregations in our Oak Park-River Forest communities are signed on to serve the other nights of the week.

"Love kindness" is essential to our walking humbly with our God. Ministry to those beneath us in social status so easily becomes patronizing. Or it is regarded as a band aid solution only. To a homeless family where the job income can't cover both food and shelter, having shelter is not a band aid solution. It's the difference between freezing or surviving through the night in these mid-winter days.

I have no desire to glamorize the human condition of those we're asked to serve. Yes, there are people with addictions, mental ailments, and bad habits of mismanagement. Yes, there is urgent need for addressing the problem at a broader community level. But for now, we are called to do what we can do. That action is better than doing nothing till brighter ideas come along.

Wonderful stories of the power of compassion are coming from surrounding congregations already at work. Guests have received job leads which have been followed up on which have meant employment sufficient to lift people out of homelessness. If you have never thought of yourself as one given undeserved help by another, think again. None of us ever makes it altogether by ourselves or of our own resources. Above all, when you and I remember the mercies of God that are new every morning, we're able to do our walk with God humbly, leaving the glory to him. Affirmations of the public importance of compassion expressed, one by one. The agnostic British curmudgeon, Bertrand Russell, said this to a Columbia University audience some years ago:

> If we want a safe and stable world, the root of the matter is a very simple and old-fashioned thing, a thing so simple that I am almost ashamed to mention it for fear of the derisive smile with which wise cynics will greet my words. The thing I mean is compassion, Christian compassion.

The time is soon at hand for us as a congregation to decide yes or no regarding this new form of mission opened up to us. It is and will be controversial. Of course. We ought to see that as a sign of our spiritual health, not sickness.

The way we get through it all, and grow in the process, is by doing justice, loving mercy, and walking humbly with our God. We get to do that—by Divine grace. It's not that we've got to in order to gain God's favor. Christ has already taken care of all that.

As people not ashamed of the Gospel nor deterred by the challenge that obeying the Gospel brings, let's do well what we are called to do in the power of God's grace that finally brings all of us—homeless as we leave this earth—home to God at last.

Partners in the Gospel
Ordination of Phyllis Kersten

December 8, 1995
Philippians 1:3-11
F. Dean Lueking, *Preacher*

I thank my God every time I remember you, constantly praying with joy in every one of my prayers for all of you, because of your sharing in the gospel from the first day until now. I am confident of this, that the one who began a good work among you will bring it to completion by the day of Jesus Christ. It is right for me to think this way about all of you, because you hold me in your heart, for all of you share in God's grace with me, both in my imprisonment and in the defense and confirmation of the gospel. For God is my witness, how I long for all of you with the compassion of Christ Jesus. And this is my prayer, that your love may overflow more and more with knowledge and full insight to help you to determine what is best, so that in the day of Christ you may be pure and blameless, having produced the harvest of righteousness that comes through Jesus Christ for the glory and praise of God. (Philippians 1:3-11)

I had become acquainted with Phyllis Kersten in the 1970s when she was on staff with LCMS World Mission and in a similar position with Wheatridge Ministries based in Chicago. I read her articles on ministry and mission with benefit and when learning of her desire to be ordained for pastoral service in urban ministry made it a point to renew our friendship. I met with her at her Chicago office on several occasions and made it known that I was thinking of her as one who could bring needed gifts to Grace Church.

Her heart was set on inner city ministry. She had served effectively in a Chicago congregation during her seminary years at the Lutheran School of Theology. I respected that priority that had grown out of her field work experience. The point I kept making was that in our unique situation Grace congregation had developed working partnerships with several inner city congregations in Chicago in addition to our primary mission to our surrounding communities. That approach seemed to win her over as an opportunity for an expanded range of service that would reach out to a diverse constituency. It made my heart glad when she agreed to consider ordination and a pastoral calling at Grace Church.

Meanwhile I had begun consultation with the elders regarding the prospect of ordaining and installing Phyllis Kersten as the first woman on our pastoral staff. This covered several months of time and included open meetings for all members to attend. I recall questions among some but not any strong opposition of note. It was heartening that a positive spirit of affirmation was the dominant response, something which came as no surprise since women had already contributed so directly as elected leaders in every office of congregation leadership.

Throughout this time of study, prayer, and listening, I made it a point to include this matter in my pastoral calls on older parishioners who were not able to attend public meetings on the subject. These were people of long years of faithful service throughout previous decades; they deserved to be heard. Again, I was grateful that most favored the thought of a woman coming to their door for pastoral calls. But not all. One woman told me bluntly: "Don't ever send a lady pastor to pray with me or give me communion." I assured her I would not. Later on, however, when word got around of what a gift Pastor Kersten was, the disgruntled parishioner found a new way to chastise me without letting on that she had changed her mind. "Why didn't you tell me beforehand that Pastor Kersten was so well qualified to serve us? . . .There you go again, getting way ahead of us without giving us a chance to know what's going on!" She delivered her admonition with a twinkle in her eye. And she gave me a hug before I left. She received Pastor Kersten gladly thereafter.

The incident belongs in describing the background for and the consequences of the following sermon which introduced the thought of an ordained woman pastor on our staff. Without doubt, there were other phone calls and parking lot conversation on the matter. That's normal and is best seen as a sign that people were interested. I did not have to be the only advocate for Phyllis Kersten's qualifications. By her own presence her gifts were soon recognized and readily appreciated. And still are today. Pastor Kersten continues now in a new role, giving generously of her abundant gifts as an interim associate pastor, coming out of retirement to help shepherd God's flock at Grace Church.

Imagine getting on the bus heading for work, sitting down next to a passenger and exclaiming with a smile, "I want you to know how glad I am to join you on the ride to work!" Or writing a letter that begins with this: "Words can't express how good it was to sit with fellow Cubs fans at Wrigley Field and join the crowd in cheering."

Even envisioning such a scenario feels awkward. Why bring it up?

Only because it contrasts so vividly with the letter I'm about to quote from and the circumstances behind it. Paul, a prisoner for the Gospel in Rome, is writing to beloved friends in the Greek city of Philippi who had sent a personal emissary with a gift all the way to Rome to assure him he was not alone. Paul had been their missionary pastor. The bond between pastor and people was stronger than ever as his opening salutation makes clear: "I thank my God in all my remembrance of you, always in every prayer of mine for you all, making my prayer with joy, thankful for your partnership in the Gospel from the first day until now." (Philippians 1:1).

Thankful for your partnership in the Gospel—that key phrase sets this sermon in motion and I want to alert you now to something of particular importance that will be said about that partnership we share at Grace.

First this: partnership is more than membership. The latter, at its lowest, mean a name on a roster, showing up at Christmas and Easter, paying dues when cash flow allows. I confess to you that I joined a Health Club some time ago—not my idea but my family's. At my first workout the instructor just about did me in, as if I was 27 instead of 57. I began skipping sessions. Here's my membership card, people, but my heart isn't in it. I'm on the verge of becoming a health club dropout.

All of us know attachments that become lightweight to say the least.

But partnership is different. This great word of the New Testament (*koinonia* if you don't mind the Greek term increasingly common among churches these days) means belonging to each other because we belong to Christ. It means participation, being a traveler on The Way, not a tourist along for the sights. It is the work of the Holy Spirit in creating the heart-to-heart kind of partnership, founded on the love that Jesus our Lord took to the cross in our behalf and by his resurrection made it good news for us forgiven sinners.

Next, partnership in the Gospel is not static but dynamic. Paul filled his letter to the Philippians with dramatic instances—read its four-chapter content later on today or before you go to bed tonight. No wonder it's called the Epistle of Joy. For many it is a favorite among the New Testament letters. I'm glad to be among them who so regard it.

I'm stating the claims of this sermon text from the pulpit. What is your experience as a partner in the Gospel at Grace Church?

Children have a way of being our teachers in such matters. In the past three months our parish school children have been digging into their pockets for their offerings for Bread for the World, for ministries that support abused kids, for the spread of the Gospel among Navaho Indians out west, for sending their words of peace—making friendship to children in the Soviet Union.

And here's important news of witness from our children of Grace who attend public schools nearby. They get to Sunday school here on Sunday mornings. Partnership to them means being a ten year old who doesn't know the others from daily friendships in the classroom. They are here nonetheless, and with their parents' guidance are forming life-long habits of practicing faith active in love. I'll give you one example. Not long ago I was visiting the home of one of our families. The 8-year-old daughter was proud to show me the large glass jar in the kitchen where she's putting in her coins week by week, learning to put her money into the collection plate at church because she's learning to whom her heart belongs.

Parents: help your children understand the importance of welcoming, befriending, playing, and working together with other children of other schools, including Grace Lutheran School. Our kids see too much television violence, bullying, and cheap humored entertainment as it is. We all are in partnership, young and old alike, to swim upstream against powerful currents that can carry us under.

Young adults belong in this subject of partnership. In a few days a group of young adults from Grace will put on a luncheon for our older adults. That takes time and effort, but ask those who do it about the joy it brings to those who are served and those who serve. The scope of functioning partnership is as high and wide and deep as Christ's love.

Being partners in the Gospel is no duty. It's all privilege, in myriad ways interacting with people in ways that bring lasting good all around.

Partnership in the Gospel endures the times and circumstance when it's tested by time and circumstance. It does take time, years of time, to begin to grasp the miracle of the many of us with all our differences growing into the deeper unity created by the Spirit of God working among us. It takes on full stature when we're upset with each other, jump to conclusions about the other one with whom we're serving, and discovering how painfully, obnoxiously clear it is that we're sinners needing God's mercies and each other's forgiveness. Yet we hold together, year and year out, because we all belong to one Lord through our one baptism by the one Spirit who unites us in the one love that outlasts everything.

Now comes this part of the sermon I mentioned before as particularly important.

In recent months I have been in study and prayerful conversation with our parish elders and congregation leaders in regard to calling an ordained woman to our pastoral staff. This has not happened before, during our nearly century-long history since our formation in 1892. It is not a step to be taken without preparation; it is not a step not to be taken because it is new. Nor is calling an ordained women something we do because the role of women in secular life is all that it is.

Why this? Why now?

Because in the mysterious ways of the Spirit's working in the church, the time becomes ripe for his breathing new life upon us in new ways. Women have always been the backbone of congregation nurture and mission. Lutherans, at least some of us, are aware of the increasing role of women in the overall well-being of the church. Here at Grace, women now occupy roles in every elected office. Women read the Scriptures in the Sunday liturgy. Women help distribute Holy Communion. And in the ministry of music and education, women continue to bless us in ways that are evident every time we hear the choirs sing or observe our Sunday school, high school, and adult education programs function.

I need additional pastoral help. I believe the depth and breadth of pastoral ministry at Grace Church can flourish to the glory of God in new ways as this step is well considered and made the consensus of the body of believers at Grace Church. I assure you that ample opportunities will be made for all of us to participate in the study of Scripture, the Lutheran theological heritage, and the timeliness of this step in our ongoing assistant pastor program at Grace Church.

And I can add with a full and grateful heart that I am aware of well-qualified women who could be a great blessing to us all if such is the will and guidance of the Lord.

As in the past, the matter of calling an ordained pastor—in this case a woman—will proceed according to our biblical base and parish constitution directives. You will be fully informed at every point as we go forward.

I hardly need to overstate the importance of prayer for God's will to be done. The enemy of our souls will jump at every chance to confuse and divide us. Oppose him stoutly.

I am glad to speak to anyone at any time on this prospect, as are our elders. Let's look forward with hope, keeping steady in faith, and remaining open to the ways in which partnership in the Gospel can have new and deeper meaning at Grace Church. Trust God to work his will among us on his timeline and in his way.

May the peace of God which passes all understanding keep our hearts and minds in Christ Jesus.

Finding a Lost Reverence for God
Trinity Sunday

June 6, 1990
Matthew 28:19
F. Dean Lueking, *Preacher*

> Go therefore and make disciples of all nations, baptizing them in the name of the Father and of the Son and of the Holy Spirit. (Matthew 28:19)

To what action of Grace Church does this sermon point? One that is primary and ongoing: encouraging gifted young people in the congregation toward a calling in the pastoral, teaching, or diaconal ministry of the church. This sermon names name several young people of Grace who are in that preparation. The local congregation is a prime location for discerning and encouraging such prospects through a timely comment that can plant the seed of an idea that the Holy Spirit then grows in the mind of a young person toward a life of service in the church. The text for this sermon is fertile ground for that seed planting. Jesus' parting word to his disciples before his ascension, often called the Great Commission, summons the church to its marching orders to take the Gospel to all nations, to baptize and teach all that Jesus has commanded.

On Trinity Sunday, the truth that is front and center is all the more important to keep front and center—the revelation of the Triune God in the face of Jesus Christ his Son. The cross Jesus carried for us is the sign of the death he endured to deliver us from sin's power. His cross is a stumbling block to our way of remedying the fix we're in. Not only the cross, but the resurrection, the ascension, and the coming of the Holy Spirit are not how humans would fashion a plan of making things right with God. The creating work of the Father, the redeeming work of the Son, the sanctifying work of the Holy Spirit—all are built into the mystery and wonder of God's reclaiming us as his redeemed children. That same thread of mystery and wonder runs through Jesus' Great Commission. He uses us, fallible and mortal as we are, as his messengers. Picture the scene as St. Matthew the Evangelist pictures it, at a mountainside in Galilee, with the disciples standing around him with no small sense of bewilderment as they are given this commission: "All authority in heaven and on earth is given unto me, go therefore to all nations and make them my disciples, baptizing them in the name of the Father and the Son and the Holy Spirit, teaching them to obey all that I have commanded you, and lo, I am with you always, to the end of the world" (Matthew 28:19).

Obedience Based in Reverence

Jesus issues a command. Not a suggestion. Nor a general religious truth. The key verb in the Great Commission is "Go!" Go means go. It means action, the action of speaking the Gospel and doing deeds that make Christ's love real. Jesus commissions his people to be about the work of discipling—which means becoming followers of Jesus. Jesus commands that people are to be baptized in the name of the Father, Son, and Holy Spirit. Such baptizing and discipling calls for teaching all that Jesus taught in his sermons, parables, judgment on sin, comfort in forgiveness, and hope in the face of death itself.

Stand back for a minute, people of Grace, and take in all that the Great Commission embodies. The marching orders are our marching orders. He means us when saying "Go" to all the world, the world that beings next door as well as extends to the ends of the earth. Stand back, I say, and marvel at what God calls us to be and to do. God the Father created us—for our part in the Great Commission. God the Son redeemed us to be partners in carrying out of the Great Commission. God the Holy Spirit is alive and at work with us in mind as the verb "Go" has our name and address on it.

If you feel that I'm getting way ahead of you in this sermon, that you wonder how you in fact fit in, don't be overwhelmed. I'm not making all this up. Gospel, baptism, disciples, teaching—are these words so foreign to you as a believer in Christ who stands with the first disciples at Jesus' ascension?

Reverence for Christ's command is the right word for the kind of obedience we seek. Not blind obedience. Nor forced obedience. Nor, indeed, neglected obedience. Reverent obedience—can you see yourself within those two words as descriptive of where you are on this Trinity Sunday morning in church? Reverence means humility, respectful, willing, teachable, open to the Holy Spirit's work. Reverence gets us beyond complacency in our present stage of discipleship as all it needs to be. Or overestimating our present stage of discipleship as well beyond what it actually is. Reverence is openness to the Lord, confidence in his grace, readiness to grow in faithful obedience and help others do the same.

In the first service this morning, a bolt of lightning hit the line into church, putting us in semi-darkness till the storm passed and the power was restored. There we all sat, surprised and suddenly aware of how easily we take for granted that the lights are on. It was an unexpected lesson in how readily we take for granted things more important than electricity.

I'm thinking of that which erodes reverence and makes it somebody else's business. The general term for it is secularism. That word is OK if it's clearly understood as moving God from the center of life to the edges. Not that God is denied altogether. Atheists, in that sense, are at least honest. The subtle danger of easing God out to the edges is that it happens so gradually and without warning. It can appear in the readiness to put human accomplishments, great as they are, into God-like importance, which they were never meant to be. Here is a thoughtful summary of the problem from an author I've not been able to name and acknowledge:

> What we have been gaping at in our world is not God. We've been gaping with admiration for the strides physical science has been making and the improvements it has brought in the material apparatus with which go about our daily business, until we have an almost completely secularized world on our hands where we learn to deal with temporal things as if they were eternal and we have no deep pervading sense of anything beyond logic and expediency in our wishful thinking. If God gets into the picture at all it is by way of being a partner down the road to some enterprise on which we have set out with very little reference to him. No corner of

our world is unexplored. We have highways, airliners, weekend tours to the wilds of Africa. . . . Everybody has leisure, yet everybody seems restless and slightly idiotic with shallow minds which are easily bored. The soul of human nature has been flattened out. The idols humanity has shaped have become its masters and civilization has gone rotten. . . .

Dear people of Grace: it's no overstatement to say that every Sunday, every gathering to hear the Word, every gathering that feeds us sacramentally for obedient discipleship is a gathering to recover again the reverence for God that gets worn thin during the week. We live in times that are anything but tranquil—drug culture, war in Vietnam, sexual morality trashed, the church dismissed, and institutions such as marriage and family treated as obsolete. . . . True enough.

But more true is this.

You have been baptized. Before being commissioned to go and baptize, you have been baptized. Your baptism and mine are not isolated events, limited to a ceremony in a church some time ago. Don't let that happen! You and all Christians were baptized into the name of the living God, the blessed and holy Trinity. In sending Jesus to die for our sins and rise again, in sending upon us the Holy Spirit in our baptism, we are commissioned to do this, and do it daily: die to sin and rise again. Dying to sin means repenting of it, turning away from it, begging God to renew Christ's grace in us day by day. Father, Son, and Holy Spirit—one God active in our daily dying and rising again—is for us. Not against us. "Lo, I am with you always" is his promise. He keeps that promise for you, for this congregation, for the whole community of faithful on earth.

When put to the test about God's keeping his promise in a given circumstance that stretches your faith to the limit, this is what to say: "Dear God, I'm wondering where you are . . . but you promised!"

Hang on to the promise. Trust God's promise even and especially when the immediate moment points otherwise.

Finding a lost reverence for God includes noticing those he calls to equip the baptized for daily ministry in the world. That's what pastors and teachers do—equip the faithful men and women and youth for mission and service day in and day out. "God gave some to be . . . pastors and teachers . . . to equip the baptized for their ministry in the world." (Ephesians 4:11 ff.)

Recognize them within our own congregation, for they are a gift to us. Robert Wetzel is leading us in worship this morning. He has completed his seminary training, is ordained, and will begin teaching this coming year at Concordia Teachers College as he completes graduate study for his specialized calling. Joel Nickel, who read the Scriptures, will spend next year as a vicar (a student intern) at an inner-city congregation in Detroit. Two young women of Grace are preparing for the teaching ministry of the church. Barbara Koehneke and Marilyn Goodman are both living signs of the Holy Trinity at work—as teachers of children in Lutheran school classrooms where children will be blessed by their gifts.

Let there be more like these! Keep your eye open when observing young people of promise active at Grace Church. Notice them, please. Get to know them. Speak encouraging words to them. Plant the seeds that can grow into full blown vocations of ministry. Grace congregation is a fertile field for planting and harvesting faithful pastors and teachers—who, in turn, equip you and me for our part in the Great Commission.

Everyone has a part in what our Lord Jesus commissioned centuries ago. From age to age the church is the workplace of the Triune God, equipping clerks, salesmen, engineers, housewives, truck drivers, judges, plumbers, doctors, steamfitters, lawyers, farmers, and all of us to take our place in the greatest work on earth: Jesus' Great Commission of making us obedient doers of his word.

Rejoice in your calling as you go out into what awaits you this week, in the name of the Father, the Son, and the Holy Spirit, to whom be all glory and praise, now and always. Amen.

Mark, the Young Man Who Fled

Lent
Mark 14:51-53
F. Dean Lueking, Preacher

A certain young man was following him, wearing nothing but a linen cloth. They caught hold of him, but he left the linen cloth and ran off naked. They took Jesus to the high priest; and all the chief priests, the elders, and the scribes were assembled. (Mark 14:51-53)

During the 1960s, mid-week Lenten sermons reached a peak in attendance, requiring two Wednesday evening Lenten services, one at 6:30 followed by another at 8:00 p.m. Among the reasons was the large number of college students from nearby Concordia Teachers College (now Concordia University Chicago) as well as the use of dialog sermons which I wrote on various figures in the Passion account in their relation to Jesus. This sermon portrays Mark the Evangelist, whose unique way of identifying himself appears in Mark 14:51-53.

EVERYMAN: It is the more careful readers of the Gospels who are familiar with the passage which leads into the theme of this sermon. Midway in St. Mark's description of Jesus' betrayal and crucifixion, he inserts two verses which seem to have little to do with the story: "And a young man followed Jesus, with nothing but a linen cloth about his body; and they seized him, but he left the linen cloth and fled away." (14:51-53)

MARK: I am that young man who fled. But not only that, I am also the man who wrote those words describing the young man who fled.

EVERYMAN: You, Mark the Evangelist, and the youth who escaped the grasp of the High Priest's palace guard, are one and the same person?

MARK: If it seems far-fetched, do not be disturbed. It is true nonetheless. This indirect reference to myself was my putting of putting my signature to the Gospel that bears my name. It was a common practice in the ancient world, just as some of your artists paint their likeness into the portrait of a crowd. It's a modest way of saying "I was there."

EVERYMAN: I've learned something new just now. Perhaps many of us have. You, Mark, the author of the second book in our New Testament, a man whom we respectfully call "Saint Mark"—you ran out on our Lord just when he needed support the most? I find that hard to believe.

MARK: It's nothing to be proud of, I assure you. All of us have turned tail and have run instead of seeing our Master through to the bitter end he met. How differently he deals with us! But—let me reset the scene of that terrible night. Maybe you will understand a little better.

You have a saying, "Boys will be boys." That was around in my day, too. I was barely into my teens when it all happened. The whole city of Jerusalem was alive with excitement. The Passover Festival had brought Jews from far and near to the City of Zion, so dear to every believer's heart. Less than a week before, Jesus had entered the city in what we thought was a triumphant parade. The word of his miraculous raising of Lazarus from the tomb in Bethany had spread through the city like wildfire. I was in the crowd that spread palm branches along his way and shouted, "Welcome, Messiah! Hosanna to the Son of David!" Oh, what a day that was! If you could know what hope filled our hearts at the thought of a deliverer at last. For decades on end we had spat in the dust as every Roman troop column marched past.

EVERYMAN: And did you hear the sermons Jesus preached each day in the temple following his entry into Jerusalem?

MARK: I only heard about them. My mother put her foot down when it came to my plea to go to the Temple court to hear him in person. My father died when I was a small child, you see, and mother has always been fretful that I would get into some needless scrape because I had no strong paternal hand over my growing up days. Here, at last, was a man of action!

EVERYMAN: We try to envision what you sensed at that fateful time. The narrow streets of Jerusalem were dark and empty. The crowded city, recently jammed with visitors for the Passover, seethes with an air of uneasiness. Suddenly the silence and darkness are broken by the loud clatter of horses and soldiers hurrying over the cobblestones. The soldiers of Caiaphas, the high priest, have taken a prisoner, delivered into their hands by torchlight in the Garden of Gethsemane. The roughnecks, hired to do their dirty work, spread the rumor which spreads like wind through the streets: "Jesus is under arrest!"

MARK: When I heard that I couldn't sit still. Mother was asleep. The curfew was on, yes, and I knew I shouldn't have been out. But what would you have done had you been in my place?

The spring air was chilly, so I reached for the first garment I could lay hands on, threw it around me and slipped through the door just in time to see the unit of the palace guard approaching. Everything was in wild confusion. But in the flicker of the torchlight I saw his face. I saw his face! His jaw was set. He was looking straight ahead. Shouts and jabs were thrown at him from every side. But it was as though he saw and hear none of it. He was silent, composed. Everyone else was excited. Not he. Surrounded by men with clubs, spears, and swords, he was still in control. I couldn't move. It was as though I was glued to the cobblestones, staring at him who was at the center of this frenzied mob.

EVERYMAN: A corporal's stripe makes many a man forget he was once a boy himself. So—there you were, shivering and alone as the mob rushed on through the streets toward the high priest's palace. Did you see what followed?

MARK: Nothing more than night. I had just picked myself up and was making my way dejectedly back to our door when another sight startled me. It was a lone figure, trailing the procession far back, crouching in every doorway and then darting ahead when no one was in sight.

EVERYMAN: And who was that?

MARK: It was Peter.

EVERYMAN: So you wrote it in the Gospel that bears your name: "And they led Jesus to the high priest and the elders and scribes. . . . And Peter followed him at a distance" (14:53-54).

MARK: The things Jesus said and did before Caiaphas and Pilate were told to me later on by Peter. I gained so much from him in writing the entire Gospel story. But I wish I could have had the nerve to have grabbed my cloak right back from the hand of that bully. If only I could have the chance to live it through all over again. Come what may, I would have stood by Jesus!

EVERYMAN: We've all thought the same thing, Mark. It's the most wistful way we can begin any sentence: "If only . . ." But the point is this: when God deals with us in Christ, he doesn't bid us look back only. Not to fix exclusively on all the grace abused, the misspent years. All that is buried in God's mercy. "Do not fear, only believe!" is Jesus word to us, as you record them in your Gospel. In Jesus, our sins are forgiven. In him there is freedom from all that all that we rightly deserve. It's not the freedom to go as before, but the freedom to start anew with God, learning to follow him by putting him first in the heart and loving the neighbor as oneself. This is what quickens the heart and moves us beyond our failed past. Though we have failed God he has not failed us. He loves sinners. And so his Don did not give up on us when all of "forsook him and fled." He went on to the cross because his strength was in God, not men. Therefore God has raised him from the tomb of death. Through the risen Jesus God sends to us and out into the world his living, Holy Spirit so that we failures might become his walking signs of what the forgiven life looks like. This is the joy and the mystery of Christian faith—that God knows all and yet forgives all.

MARK: To that we say a heartfelt "Yes." But I must tell you that I lived many years before the full power of that truth began to truly take hold of my life. All of you might not know it, but there are further references in me in the New Testament. You need to see the whole picture of my days in order to get the real message of what I wrote down in the Gospel.

EVERYMAN: The evangelist Luke speaks of you several times in the Book of Acts. The first glimpse we get of you is a dozen or so years after that night of Jesus' betrayal. We learn that your full name was John Mark. Moreover, we read that you were still living in Jerusalem with your mother, whose name was Mary. Both of you followers of The Way. Your cousin, Barnabas, one of the most notable figures in the early church. And this is the striking thing: the apostle Paul selected you, together with Barnabas, to join him on his first missionary journey.

MARK: Notable indeed! I was in my late twenties by then. The first dozen verses of Acts 12 tells of the fast pace of missionary labors Paul set for us as we began proclaiming the Gospel on the island of Cyprus. Read that account. In it you'll find not only the record of our adventures as fledgling missionaries, but you will also find the verse that tells you I left the company of Paul and Barnabas as soon as we landed on the coast of southern Turkey.

EVERYMAN: Here's the verse, so brief, so cryptic: "And John Mark left them and returned to Jerusalem" (Acts 13:13). What caused you to do that, Mark, just when your missionary journey was getting well started?

MARK: Luke, that true gentleman, shielded my motives. Many have sought to find out why I left for home. This is one more secret that you must leave to heaven. But two things are obvious enough. First, the southern coast of Turkey is a wild and forbidding area. Everything from malaria to wild animals made the going impossibly difficult. And then you must not forget that I had my widowed mother in Jerusalem to think of. . . . You see how easy it is to begin to rationalize, to explain, to justify. No, there is a third reason for my leaving which is one you know about. It is shrinking away from costly discipleship. I could see then what Paul and Barnabas did see, that God supplies the need as well as the demand. I went back, alone and miserable, while Paul and Barnabas went ahead in faith to plant the seed which became the Galatian churches.

EVERYMAN: And then what happened to you, Mark?

MARK: You do well to read it yourself in the last verses of Acts 15. Paul and Barnabas were making plans for their second missionary journey, one which would take them all the way west to Athens and Corinth. Barnabas, who was my cousin, remember, proposed that I would be ready to stay with the cause this time. That open-minded cousin of mine! But Paul said "No." And when Paul said "No," there was no arguing with the man. Again, Luke deals gently with the matter when he summarized Paul's reason: "Paul thought it best not to take with them one who had withdrawn from them in Pamphylia, and had not gone with them to the work" (Acts 15:38). The division was so sharp between Paul and Barnabas that they did the necessary thing—parted ways, each going on separately, Barnabas took me with him to revisit and strengthen the church of Cyprus. Paul took Silas through Galatia to Greece.

EVERYMAN: Your experience brings home an all too familiar point, Mark. Once a man gets the reputation for being a quitter and a weakling, it's hard to change that impression. One weak moment of indecision at a crucial turning point can take years to repair, and who can measure the misery and loss suffered by Christians who missed the opportune moment for faithful discipleship and had to endure the consequences?

MARK: May God be thanked, that's not the last word on my life. Nor yours. Although Paul did not think well of me after that fiasco in southern Turkey, the breach between us was healed toward the end of our lives. When Paul wrote one of his last epistles, the letter to the Colossians, he was in prison in Rome. I had met him there. We were reconciled!

EVERYMAN: There is one more glimpse of Mark in the New Testament, one that comes toward the end of his life. It is a moment that shows what happens when God has the last word, the word of grace and forgiveness. Mark is on his way to Colosse to serve the congregation there. He has a work to do and fellow workmen with whom to share it. Mark is, at last, really a saint—in the basic meaning of the word—a forgiven sinner who knows it and lives it. Paul puts into his letter to the Colossian Christians a little comment implying something very great that has happened. "Aristarchus, Christ's servant like myself, sends his greetings, so does Mark, the cousin of Barnabas (you have received instructions about him, when he comes make him welcome)." . . . (Colossians 4:10)

What do you think those instructions were? Surely they told of how a young man who fled, who walked away from the work, who then had a second chance—and took it. Now, his hand is to the plow and his heart is set on doing the work of an evangelist. He brings to his renewed calling a maturity that comes from humbling himself and letting God lift him up.

Mark's story is the key to our story. God uses mortals, not angels for his work on earth. That is ever and always miraculous—that in spite of all that's wrong with us, the Lord Jesus sets us right and gives us a place in what the church is called to do: build each other up and take the Good News out into the world that needs it.

Thanks be to God, now and evermore!

Sermons
By *Bruce K. Modahl*

Getting Bent into Shape: A Call for Reformation
Reformation Sunday

October 30, 2005
John 8:31-36
Bruce K. Modahl, *Preacher*

Then Jesus said to the Jews who had believed in him, "If you continue in my word, you are truly my disciples; and you will know the truth, and the truth will make you free." They answered him, "We are descendants of Abraham and have never been slaves to anyone. What do you mean by saying, 'You will be made free'?" Jesus answered them, "Very truly, I tell you, everyone who commits sin is a slave to sin. The slave does not have a permanent place in the household; the son has a place there forever. So if the Son makes you free, you will be free indeed. (John 8:31-36)

The Christian Church in America is as polarized as our society. We hear talk of red state and blue state. The church is increasingly divided along the same color lines. I preached this sermon out of the conviction that red church/blue church is not the church. We are in need of a new reformation that would follow the same contours as the Reformation in the sixteenth century. As you read the sermon keep in mind that the conference to which I make reference and the sermon I preached date from 2005, in the first year of George W. Bush's second term as president.

A friend came into town to go with me to a five-day preaching conference. This event is held every year. The host churches are large, old, Gothic places located in the heart of major cities. Close to 1,000 pastors come from all over the country. The participants are Methodist, Presbyterian, United Church of Christ, some Lutherans and Episcopalians, and a smattering of Catholics. It is a preaching conference for the mainline or old-line churches. The less kind call it the sideline.

On the political spectrum my friend is just to the right of Rush Limbaugh. He considers Bill O'Reilly a moderate. He started squirming right away on Monday because of the constant potshots taken at the current administration in Washington. [Remember, this is in 2005.] The potshots coming from the dais were one thing. But with every potshot the people all around us sniggered, applauded and laughed. To a speaker that sort of response from an audience is gas on the fire so they gave us more of it. I don't share my friend's political views. I thought many of the potshots taken at George Bush were funny. But it got to the point that I had to check the program to see if this was indeed a preaching conference or had we wandered into a Moveon.org convention. One speaker compared the neocons and fearmongers in Washington to the Siths, the scary species in the latest Star Wars episode. One lecture was entitled "Preaching across Differences." But even that presenter spent a good bit of her time ridiculing right-wing religious leaders. "Tune in to 'Feeling the Hate' with the National Religious Broadcasters," she quipped. And when she actually got to the point of addressing those who have different opinions on politics and social issues her advice amounted to pointers on how to enlighten those in the dark and open closed minds. Two days into this and during one particularly partisan lecture my friend leaned into me and said, "I don't know that I belong here."

At big-box churches in the suburbs, the antithesis of mainline Gothic, pastors gather for similar events. Only these are from the other end of the religious-political spectrum. A speaker at one such gathering said, "If we have to give equal time to every opposing viewpoint there would be no time to proclaim the truth." And then he mocked liberal Christians by adopting a lisping, limp-wristed voice. Using that voice he said, "Those who want to share and be sensitive to the needs of others are wrong." The place erupted in applause and laughter. If my friend and I attended that conference I would be the one leaning into him and saying, "I don't think I belong here."

Something is wrong here. What constitutes our belonging is being in Christ by faith. We are baptized into Christ. That is not what seems to matter. Something is wrong here. What forms the church is the Gospel, the good news that we are justified, that is declared righteous, by God's grace, by God's free gift, through faith in Jesus Christ. The Holy Spirit forms the church by that Gospel. Luther said the Holy Spirit uses the Gospel to "call, gather, enlighten, sanctify and keep us." The image that comes to mind is a lump of clay with the cross pressed into it. That is the shape we are in. But the churches gathered in these disparate places seem to be formed by something else. Something is bending the church out of shape. Triumphalism does it. Triumphalism is, "We are saved and they are not. We are right and they are stupid." Triumphalism is incompatible with the cross. It distorts the cross. It bends the church out of shape today just as certainly as it bent the church out of shape in Luther's day.

What bends the church out of shape is adding something to the Gospel. "Yes, we believe Jesus Christ was crucified and raised for our salvation. But if you expect to be saved, if you really want to be a Christian then you must do enough good works or buy enough indulgences to cancel out your sin." That is what bent the church out of shape in Luther's day.

In the first century some representatives from the bishop's office in Jerusalem came to visit the churches in Galatia and found they were ignoring some of the Old Testament laws. They said, "We believe Jesus was crucified and raised for our salvation but if you expect to be saved, if you really want to live as God's people then you must also be circumcised and observe the dietary laws." That is what bent the church out of shape in Paul's day.

Nowadays, we hear, in effect, "We believe in Jesus Christ crucified and raised for our salvation but if we are to be right with God and with one another, if we want to live as Christians then we must also hold to this particular set of opinions on the current political and social issues. If you want to belong here that is what you must do." This is what is bending the church out of shape in our day so that some will say, "I don't belong here."

It happens by adding something to the Gospel. That addition is the hallmark of triumphalism. When we add something to the Gospel we are in effect saying, "Jesus' death and resurrection are not enough." The issue here goes far beyond being civil with those with whom we disagree. The problem goes much deeper than our civic life. When we add something to the Gospel we belittle Christ's work on the cross. We rob the cross of Christ of its power. We offend God.

The church is bent out of shape and needs reform. It needs to be bent back into shape. The Holy Spirit uses the Gospel to reform us. There is pain involved. Getting bent into shape hurts. The truth hurts, we say. First and foremost Jesus is the truth. We see hurt looming before us at the cross. It hurts to admit that our sin requires nothing less than the death of God's Son. Our brokenness requires a crucified and risen savior. The truth convicts us of the fact. The truth humbles us. It frees us from any notion of our own righteousness. And it frees us from any notion that we are worthless. God in Jesus became one of us. We are so filled with worth in God's sight that he gave his Son for us. We recognize our own worth in the face of Jesus. The truth opens up to us the new world of the kingdom of God in which we live with one another not by being right but by God's grace. By God's grace we are managers of God's mercy in our daily lives and so extend God's kingly rule day by day into new territory. As Christ humbled himself, we practice humility with each other. As Christ sought and loved and called and welcomed all to new life, so do we. This does not mean we avoid discussing difficult issues. On the contrary I think because we are secure in Christ we are free to do so. My friend and I discuss and argue and sometimes we have to apologize to each other for the way we have expressed ourselves. But we stand next to each other in worship, embrace when it is time to share the peace and come one behind the other with our hands extended as the beggars we are for the bread of life in Holy Communion.

Wesley Wildman wrote, "When the going gets tough and worldview conflicts cause fights, that's the time to retell the old, old story ("When Narrative Identities Clash," *Congregation*, Fall, 2005). We tell how Jesus overcame the biggest barrier of all, the one between God and us. We tell how Paul engaged in the hard work of gathering so many different kinds of people into Christian communities. These were people who otherwise would not have anything to do with one another. But in Christ, Paul said, there is no longer slave and free, male and female, Jew and Gentile. And while we might have red state and blue state, red church-blue church is not the church. Red church-blue church is the church bent out of shape.

It is time once again for reformation.

A Time to Mourn

Fifteenth Sunday after Pentecost

September 16, 2001
Luke 15:1-10
Bruce K. Modahl, Preacher

Now all the tax collectors and sinners were coming near to listen to him. And the Pharisees and the scribes were grumbling and saying, "This fellow welcomes sinners and eats with them." So he told them this parable: "Which one of you, having a hundred sheep and losing one of them, does not leave the ninety-nine in the wilderness and go after the one that is lost until he finds it? When he has found it, he lays it on his shoulders and rejoices. And when he comes home, he calls together his friends and neighbors, saying to them, 'Rejoice with me, for I have found my sheep that was lost.' Just so, I tell you, there will be more joy in heaven over one sinner who repents than over ninety-nine righteous persons who need no repentance."

"Or what woman having ten silver coins, if she loses one of them, does not light a lamp, sweep the house, and search carefully until she finds it? When she has found it, she calls together her friends and neighbors, saying, 'Rejoice with me, for I have found the coin that I had lost.' Just so, I tell you, there is joy in the presence of the angels of God over one sinner who repents." (Luke 15:1-10)

I preached this sermon on the Sunday following the terrorist attack on our country. An explanatory note is necessary. I say in the sermon that what is not assumed cannot be redeemed. I am quoting theologians from the early centuries of the church. By assume I do not mean an assumption based on evidence or guesswork. Assume in the context of this sermon means to take into one's hands. For example we say, "I assumed the task," or "I assumed his debts."

The Prayer of the Day says that God declares almighty power chiefly in showing mercy and pity. Almighty power is mercy and pity? That claim seems at odds with the events of this past week. That claim seems out of keeping with the kind of almighty power we need from God.

I have heard it said that God did this or at least allowed it to happen because we as a nation have strayed from God. This is our punishment. I don't believe that for a minute, not even a New York minute. I know we can find passages in the Bible in which we are told God punishes Israel with a military defeat. But to say that is the same with us is to equate our nation with the Israel of the Old Testament. We are not the messianic nation.

It is not that Scripture offers us no help in interpreting the events of this past week. The prophet Joel for one is great help. When calamity strikes the nation, he announces a time of mourning, "Call a solemn assembly. Proclaim a fast. King and commoner dress in sack cloth and ashes," he says. He even calls for repentance, a turning to God. He does so not because the calamity is God's punishment for some particular thing. Rather, the tragedy, he says, confronts us with how fragile we are, how much in need of God we are. The prophet Isaiah, after a big defeat, tells the people, "Put not your trust in chariots because they are strong and in horsemen because they are many. Put your trust in the Lord your God." This is a time to mourn those who died, a time to mourn our brokenness. This tragedy compels our turning to God. Wall Street is not God. Neither is our military might, certainly not the terrorists. We resolve to trust our lives to the Lord our God.

When the prophets called the people to a time of mourning, they sang psalms of lament. Last Thursday during Confirmation our youth wrote such psalms. Here is what one of them wrote: "I gave my heart to you, O Lord, and you handled it with care. But now, O Lord, I am most troubled. I need you to hold it close. I need to know, to understand why innocent people have died." Another wrote: "Dear God, I have so many feelings inside of me, none of which I know how to put down. I'm so confused. Please help me through this terrible time." And another: "My heart is like the wind howling, always circling, moving between faith and hopeless doubting, fear and strong belief for I am frightened.

. . . Restore me by the blood of the lamb that fear will have no power, that my soul may rest peacefully in your firm grasp." Like the laments in the Old Testament, they ended each psalm with a statement of trust in God. Our time of mourning rests upon our trust in God.

That begs, however, the issue of God's power and presence in this situation. Where was God and what was God doing last Tuesday? That question begs the larger issue of the agency of God in this created order. How is God present and how does God operate? And you'd like the answer in ten minutes, right? Well, a beginning at least.

In the beginning, before God spoke the first things into being, God filled the whole cosmos. The material creation is from God but is not God. That means God had to make room for what God created. God pulled in, as it were, to make room. The analogy I use is of a family. In the beginning of a marriage the couple fills every cubic inch of the space they occupy. They withdraw from some of that space to make room for their creation. They decorate a nursery. Then they outfit a playroom. Sometimes they have to assert themselves to prevent the whole house from being taken over. Children also are not puppets on the parents' string. That never works. God's creation is good. God's human creation is very good, God says.

Something went wrong with that good creation. Something tore at our relationship with God. This past week Jesse Jackson said, "The terrorists have tried to tear us apart from one another." If that is the definition of a terrorist, then the first terrorists were the first human beings. As a result of that tear, suffering is humanity's lot. It goes with the territory of being human. This territory is bounded all around by death whether that comes at a ripe old age or suddenly in a terrorist strike. So this is territory occupied by a fallen humanity. It is occupied territory, torn away from its rightful Lord and under an alien lordship, the power of evil. In this occupied territory how does God exercise God's power? We say God exercises that power through the law. God rules through civil authorities. Whether they acknowledge God or not, God rules through them. God rules to restrain evil and promote the common good. So shall God rule also in this situation in seeking justice by identifying those responsible, bringing them to account, and punishing them based on the evidence.

This is God's power at work. God works through means. We shall not see God's unvarnished power, God's unveiled face, or God's ungloved hand in this world. And it is not God's almighty power. If this were God's ultimate power that would mean God's final power is the power of the sword. Should God exercise ultimate power in this venue, then why would God stop at wiping out the terrorists before they could seize control of the airplanes? If the first terrorists were Adam and Eve, they passed the sickness to their children. A man told me that at his Alcoholics Anonymous meeting this week one person said to the group, "We are terrorists. We terrorized our spouses, our children. We terrorized our coworkers and everyone close to us. We killed innocents in our drunken state. We were willing to kill ourselves by continuing to drink." If God were to exercise almighty power through the law, God would have to wipe out the whole business and start over. That was God's first impulse in the first reading today. But the law is not the only power, and it is not God's almighty power. The Gospel is. God chooses not to wipe out but to redeem the whole business, to turn wayward Israel back to God, to transform Paul's life, to seek and save the lost as we heard in the Gospel reading.

What is not assumed, however, is not redeemed. So God assumes the whole business. In Jesus Christ God takes the brokenness of the whole world to himself in order to redeem the whole world. Here again God works through means. We see God's almighty power at work wherever there is suffering. We see God's almighty power at work in the rescue and recovery efforts in New York and at the Pentagon. The Gospel reading describes joy when the lost is found. I saw on the news a woman who had been on the way with her husband to the World Trade Center when the tragedy struck. They were separated in the mayhem that followed. Was he dead? Where was he? Walking along the street, they spot each other. Oh, what joy! Sgt. John McLoughlin, a twenty-one-year veteran of the Port Authority police, was pulled alive from under 40 feet of rubble after surviving almost twenty-four hours. His legs were broken. He was entangled in the metal cables that bind cement. The rescuers formed a human chain. When they finally reached him, the cheer rose but quickly fell. The work continued in the ruins. At the service last Wednesday night I read from Bishop Stephen Bouman's letter from New York City. Steve is a son of this congregation and is bishop of the Metro New York Synod. In a part of that letter he wrote: "A member of Bethlehem in the Bronx worked on the forty-second floor of the World Trade Center. They were able to evacuate all of those in her office. She is wheelchair bound, and we have not heard from her." In his letter from the next day he writes, "About the lady from the Bronx in the wheelchair . . . an unnamed man carried her all the way down to safety. Amid the chaos, she was somewhere in lower Manhattan. We give thanks for the fragments of resurrection from the ashes." Here and through these rescuers is the power of God at work seeking and saving the lost.

Some of these lambs, however, will not be found alive. Some of these lambs will not be found at all, at least not by human hands. What the rescue workers know is that to lift a heavy load you have to get under it, all the way under it. It is dangerous work. And so when God would raise up rather than destroy the whole fallen world, God's first act was one of descent. In Jesus Christ God put himself under the weight of this whole world. On the cross Jesus bears that weight. God raises his Son to life, the foundation of a redeemed creation.

We, like those rescue workers in New York City have a part to play in flexing God's almighty power. There is an effort afoot here by the Women of Grace to organize support for Lutheran Social Services in New York City. We are working at establishing partner relationships with Lutheran churches and schools in the affected area. Already we have received $10,000. Someone else has offered to match our additional offerings dollar for dollar up to $10,000. The fourth graders of Grace School tied crosses around the old oak tree out front and the elm and the birch and the silver maple. The school chapel offerings will be devoted to disaster relief. There is much that needs relief. Steve told me that in one Lutheran school alone twenty children have parents missing and presumed dead in this tragedy. The confirmands wrote laments. We have gathered three times this past week to mourn. Our mourning is part of the groaning of God's creation for redemption. This groaning, this mourning too is an expression of God's almighty power.

The Sentinel's Cry

Sixteenth Sunday after Pentecost

The First Anniversary of September 11, 2001
Ezekiel 33:7-11
Bruce K. Modahl, Preacher

So you, mortal, I have made a sentinel for the house of Israel; whenever you hear a word from my mouth, you shall give them warning from me. If I say to the wicked, "O wicked ones, you shall surely die," and you do not speak to warn the wicked to turn from their ways, the wicked shall die in their iniquity, but their blood I will require at your hand. But if you warn the wicked to turn from their ways, and they do not turn from their ways, the wicked shall die in their iniquity, but you will have saved your life.

Now you, mortal, say to the house of Israel, Thus you have said: "Our transgressions and our sins weigh upon us, and we waste away because of them; how then can we live?" Say to them, As I live, says the Lord God, I have no pleasure in the death of the wicked, but that the wicked turn from their ways and live; turn back, turn back from your evil ways; for why will you die, O house of Israel? (Ezekiel 33:7-11)

I have been reading about and hearing about the various events planned to commemorate 9/11. Or more precisely, to commemorate those who died and honor the heroes who died in the rescue effort, to thank members of our armed forces and reserves, to recognize those who toiled twelve-hour days seven days a week to recover the dead and clear the destruction, those who counseled and prayed and held hands, those who are still in need of having their hands held, and those who continue to extend the holding hand. I have been reading about and hearing about the various events planned to address all of that.

9/11/01 was a gorgeous Tuesday morning. We will always remember where we were and what we were doing on that day. I was at a breakfast meeting. On my way back to church I remember exulting in the beauty of the day. I can still picture the drive from Lake Street to here. When I arrived Pastor Kersten told me what she had heard on the radio as she drove from the meeting. I went to the *New York Times* web page on the internet and saw the first pictures of the awful events of the day. Terrorists commandeered four passenger planes, turned them into missiles, and flew them into the two towers of the World Trade Center in New York City and the Pentagon in Northern Virginia. Where the fourth plane was headed we will never know for sure. Perhaps the White House or the Capitol. Heroic passengers fought back, and in the struggle the plane crashed in rural Pennsylvania. Terrorists murdered 3,000 people that day.

On Wednesday of this week, 9/11/02, and in the days around it, at a variety of events our civic and secular leaders are going to read Abraham Lincoln's *Gettysburg Address* and the *Declaration of Independence* penned largely by Thomas Jefferson. Some leaders will read the preamble to the *Constitution of the United States*. These are worthy texts. They are foundational for who we are as a nation. But do these leaders have nothing of their own to say? I don't mean to be hard on them. I don't think it is their fault. I think there simply is no longer a common language or vocabulary available to our culture as a whole that is able to do anything more than narrate events. To be sure, the events of 9/11/01 and the days following must be narrated, the story told, and remembered. But we need more than that. We yearn for more. Unfortunately we no longer have even a passing fluency in a language that can give transcendent dimensions to these events. We can only fall back on another time and mimic those who did have the language necessary. As we commemorate the events of 9/11/01, the community will be without words of its own.

Not that silence is inappropriate—silence and heads bowed in prayer. In fact silence alone would be preferable by far to the wrong words. The only thing worse than not having words is to speak diabolic ones. We learned that last week when Peter spoke his objections to Jesus' cross. It was then we found out what other kind of rock Peter can be.

Jesus named him Rock. That's what Peter means. Jesus named him that because he is the foundation stone upon which Jesus builds his church. But we found out in the walking-on-water incident that Peter is also sinking stone. Last week we discovered he can be a stone of stumbling as well. To stumbling Peter Jesus said, "Get behind me Satan." Strong words. So silence is far preferable to speaking words that are demonic.

I learned about this from reading Elie Wiesel. He experienced a different kind of terror. He is a holocaust survivor. He was a teenager in the Nazi concentration camps. He wrote a play about yet another experience of terror. His play is set in a town in Czarist Russia. The terror is a pogrom against the Jews of the community. The Jews left alive gather at the inn belonging to Berish. His wife was murdered. His daughter was violated and now is out of her mind. A Jewish theater troop comes to the village. They know nothing of the pogrom. It is Purim, the Jewish holiday related to the book of Esther, one rare time when the Jewish people triumph over their oppressors. On Purim it is customary to perform plays and wear masks. Berish forbids any such gaiety. The only play he will agree to is if they will stage a trial. He wants to put God on trial for allowing his innocent people to suffer. They agree. Berish will be prosecuting attorney. No one is willing to be God's defense attorney until a stranger shows up. He mounts all the usual defenses for God and explanations of evil.

- It was God's will. Who are you to question God?
- They did something to deserve it. There was some justification for God to send this terror as a punishment.
- God didn't do it directly, but God allowed it to happen. God stood by, hands in pockets.
- They are now in a better place.
- There is a reason for it that you will know at some time.
- They have been spared even worse problems.
- God needed them in heaven more than we needed them on earth.

These are the arguments. We have heard them. We have even given voice to some of them. At the very end of the trial, the mob comes and begins to break into the inn to kill these last remaining Jews. They decide to put on the Purim masks and so greet the murderous crowd. The defense attorney puts on his, and it is the mask of Satan. Wiesel's meaning is clear. The standard defenses for God and explanations of evil are demonic. In the face of such profound evil, silence with heads bowed in prayer is the appropriate response. That's how the Jews in Berish's inn met their deaths. That is how, in part, we shall respond at our own service this Wednesday.

And yet after the silence we want a word. We yearn for a word that is more than a narration of what happened. We crave a word from God. For that purpose God appoints a sentinel and a watchtower. The watchtower is this pulpit; the sentinel, those who stand within. May the words spoken from the watchtowers in our land not be stumbling blocks. God has entrusted to us the keys to the kingdom. As the anniversary of 9/11/01 approaches, to what would we bind and from what would we loose? We bind ourselves to the promises of God. The word of God unlocks us from our fear.

The language in which we seek fluency is this Scripture. The word from the sentinel's post requires also a text. The text I believe God has placed in my hands is this parable of Jesus'. I am in debt to Tom Long for the interpretation of this psalm.

A landowner sowed good seed in his field. But while everyone was asleep an enemy came and sowed weeds among the wheat and then went away. So when the plants came up and bore grain the weeds sprouted as well. And the employees of that landowner came and said to him, "Master, we thought you planted good seed in the field. Where did these weeds come from?" The owner answered, "An enemy has done this." The workers said, "Do you want us to go into the field and pull up the weeds." The owner said, "No, because in doing that you will pull up some of the good plants and you won't get all the weeds anyway. Let's wait until the harvest. I'll tell the harvest workers (always the angels in Jesus' parables) to collect the weeds first and tie them in bundles to be burned and then gather the wheat into my barn."

Jesus tells the parable out of pastoral concern for those who have seen evil at work, who have experienced some tragic loss. He tells this parable for parents whose baby dies, for Elie Wiesel who lived through the kingdom of the night, for those who read Wiesel's book *Night* and yearn with him for a word from God about the justice of God. Jesus tells the parable for those who watched the towers fall at the World Trade Center, hauled bodies out of Ground Zero, attended too many funeral services, and held the hands of too many victims.

"Did God do this?" No. God planted good seed. God's creation is good. An enemy did this.

"Can we do anything about it?" No. We are not going to do away with evil. We have to be careful with this one because Jesus is not implying we stand with our hands in our pockets in the face of evil. We hear of drug dealers in the park, an abusive spouse, corrupt politicians and respond, "Can't do anything about such things. We'll always have those sorts of problems. If we try to weed out the bad ones we might do some harm to the good that is there." That is not the conclusion to draw from this parable. God does not give us sentinels the option of being hands-in-pockets bystanders. But are we going to rid the world of evil? No.

The third question: "Will it always be this way?" No. The time is coming. John saw and reported to us,

> I saw a new heaven and a new earth… the new Jerusalem, coming down out of heaven from God, prepared as a bride adorned for her husband. And I heard a loud voice from the throne saying, "See, the home of God is among mortals…. He will wipe every tear from their eyes. Death will be no more; mourning and crying and pain will be no more…. " And the one who was seated on the throne said, "See, I am making all things new."

The One seated on the throne is Immanuel, God with us, Jesus, by whose death and resurrection the new creation is born. We live out of that hope. We act out that future even in a weed-infested world.

Keep Us from Presumptuous Sins
Third Sunday in Lent

March 23, 2003
Psalm 19:13; John 2:13-22
Bruce K. Modahl, Preacher

Keep back your servant also from presumptuous sins; let them not have dominion over me! Then I shall be blameless, and innocent of great transgression. (Psalm 19:13, ESV).

The Passover of the Jews was near, and Jesus went up to Jerusalem. In the temple he found people selling cattle, sheep, and doves, and the money changers seated at their tables. Making a whip of cords, he drove all of them out of the temple, both the sheep and the cattle. He also poured out the coins of the money changers and overturned their tables. He told those who were selling the doves, "Take these things out of here! Stop making my Father's house a marketplace!" His disciples remembered that it was written, "Zeal for your house will consume me." The Jews then said to him, "What sign can you show us for doing this?" Jesus answered them, "Destroy this temple, and in three days I will raise it up." The Jews then said, "This temple has been under construction for forty-six years, and will you raise it up in three days?" But he was speaking of the temple of his body. After he was raised from the dead, his disciples remembered that he had said this; and they believed the scripture and the word that Jesus had spoken. (John 2:13-22)

I preached this sermon on the Sunday following the invasion of Iraq. The text from the psalm appointed for the day is from the Common Worship Psalter, included in the Lutheran Book of Worship (LBW) and the Book of Common Prayer (BCP), among others.

The psalmist prays, "Above all keep your servant from presumptuous sins." I am confident that across America today there are those who will stand up in their pulpits and compare Jesus' cleansing of the temple in Jerusalem to the task the U.S. military has undertaken in Iraq, cleansing the country of evildoers. I am not one of them. I say rather, "keep your servants from presumptuous sins."

I recognize that this applies to me. I have never liked sermons that delve into politics unless, of course, the preacher's politics agree with my own. But it is not what sermons are for. I read the sermons Dietrich Bonhoeffer preached in the concentration camp to the little group that gathered clandestinely for worship. His sermons are pastoral and evangelical. They comfort and they preach Christ. He even prays for the governing authorities. Outside the pulpit he expressed many opinions and even engaged in a plot on Hitler's life. But that was outside the pulpit. Politics in the pulpit make it a bully pulpit. There is no dialogue here. The word spoken from this mouth and from this place is to be a word from God. Today God will be for the war from some pulpits and against it in others. Keep us, O Lord, from presumptuous sins.

I recall a discussion I had with someone during the Viet Nam war. I said I thought it was possible that one person out of Christian conviction would don the uniform of our country and fight and another person out of Christian conviction could be a conscientious objector and refuse to fight. My dialogue partner said, "No, the only Christian response is to obey our country's call and go to war. It says so in Romans 13," and he quoted, "Let every person be subject to the governing authorities; for there is no authority except from God, and those authorities that exist have been instituted by God." Recently I heard those words applied to our president. He has his authority from God to do what he is doing, this person said. Maybe it is not as simple as that. Paul writes about pagan Rome. By Paul's logic in Romans 13, Saddam Hussein also has authority from God. But that wasn't the line I took with my dialogue partner. And let me be honest. By now it was a heated discussion. No, to be totally honest it was a full-blown, red-faced, heated-words argument. He quoted Romans. I quoted Acts 5, Peter before the council in Jerusalem: "We must obey God rather than any human authority." There. I'm right. You're wrong.

I read a definition of war this past week. I saw it in the Sunday comics of all places. The cartoon is called "Non Sequitur." I don't read the comics very often, so I don't know who the characters are. A man and a little girl are out walking a dog. The little girl says, "Sometimes I wonder how we got words. Like where does 'war' come from?" The man says, "It's a universal acronym." "An acronym of what?" she asks. "We are right," he responds. WAR, We Are Right. Above all, O Lord, keep your servants from presumptuous sins.

Presuming we are right puts us at odds with each other. The problem is much worse when we presume to speak for God or to act on God's behalf. We are treading on first commandment territory, arrogating God's prerogatives to ourselves. We are trespassing also on second commandment turf. For when we use God's name to justify our words and actions, then we are taking God's name in vain in a way that is far more serious than a frivolous, "Oh, God."

I was astonished to hear one commentator, I don't know if this person was a government spokesman or from the media, using the messianic language of Isaiah. He described the coming conflict as making a way in the wilderness to liberate the oppressed. A *New York Times* reporter described the bombing of Baghdad as being of biblical proportions.[1] What proportions would those be? The plagues on Egypt? Fire and brimstone on Sodom and Gomorrah? Keep us, O Lord, from presumptuous sins.

In a recent newspaper column in the *Wall Street Journal,* the author points out that biblical Israel's enemy was Babylon and Babylon is modern-day Iraq. He further points out that immigrants to this country often interpreted their experience in biblical terms. They were the new Israel coming in to settle the Promised Land, America. Sermons along the frontier in the nineteenth century are filled with this kind of language. And there was much good in that. It gave people comfort, hope, and endurance to see themselves in biblical terms. But it's not that simple. It also gave warrant to some to justify displacing Native Americans. If the settlers were the New Israel, then the Indians were the Canaanites. And I am assuming the author knows that those brought

---

[1] John F. Burns, "A Staggering Blow Strikes at the Heart of the Iraqi Capital," *New York Times,* 3/22/03, A1.

to this country in chains and stacked like cord wood in the holds of slave ships did not interpret their immigrant experience with quite the same triumphal imagery. But that's another story. Israel versus Babylon, America versus Iraq, good versus evil is the pattern this author derives from biblical history. The author says, "Scripture sets down paradigms in which we ourselves live our lives. . . . If the Bible helps us understand the patterns that drive history, that would mean that in its pages we find not fantasy but reality, by which a wise leader should indeed be guided [in seeking war]."[2] Keep us, O God, from presumptuous sins.

And maybe it is not as simple as this writer makes it out to be. The prophet Jeremiah does not call Babylon part of an axis of evil. He said Babylon was God's appointed agent for punishing idolatrous Israel. Furthermore, the patterns set down in Scripture do not drive history. God drives history. God is sovereign and is not tied to a pattern. There is, however, a rhythm of God's interaction with us that we can discern from Scripture and from our own experience. The rhythm is judgment and grace. God's first word to us is a critical word. I discovered the critical word when I was looking through the Old Testament for how else this word, presumption, is used. In Deuteronomy 18:20 God says, "Any prophet [that is anyone] who presumes to speak in my name a word that I have not commanded the prophet to speak—that prophet shall die." There's the critical word, the word of judgment. What is the graceful word that will cancel out our presumption, cross it out of our lives? That word is humility. But we are not going to get it on our own. The word of judgment comes from God. The graceful word shall have to come from God as well. Look to the one who is God's Word.

Jesus encountered presumption at the temple in Jerusalem. He has a run in with those who ran the place, who found in the temple the immutable pattern of history for how God deals with God's people. What Jesus does there has nothing to do with the sale of Girl Scout cookies in the narthex. And what Jesus was about was not the reform of Temple worship either. It was not a cleansing. He overturned the whole pattern, the entire old paradigm. He comes to replace the temple as the locus of God's presence among us. He replaces it with himself. Those who ran the place presumed to know God's will. That pre-

---

2 David Klinghoffer, "Babylon Revisited," *Wall Street Journal*, 3/14/03.

sumption blinded their eyes and stopped up their ears so they did not recognize their Lord when he suddenly appeared in the temple, as the prophet Malachi said he would. And it would lead them to worse than that. Presumption will cause them to put him to death. Jesus answered presumption with humility, a humility that was strangely authoritative. He is the only and best hope also for presumptuous chief priests and scribes. They ask Jesus for a sign, a signal, a biblical warrant that would justify his actions. The warrant Jesus offers is his own humility. Raze this temple, Jesus says, referring to his own body. And they will. Raze this temple, and in three days I will raise it up. Jesus complains that they have made his Father's house a marketplace. He offers himself as the marketplace, the place where God trades with us, our presumption for Jesus' humility. Chief priest and scribal presumption, even ours is razed to the ground with him. And with him we are raised to new life, living out of the benefits of his humility.

This authoritative humility of Jesus frees us to acknowledge the ambiguity of the decisions we must make. Most of our decisions are made between a rock and a hard place. The decision to go to war is one of these. The choices we have are seldom as simple as some would make them out to be. We make our decisions prayerfully. We seek God's will and the direction of the Holy Spirit. But we must always acknowledge that we may be wrong. We do not have God in our back pockets.

May our response to this war not be exaltation at the humiliation of Iraqis. The proper biblical response is lament even as Jesus lamented over Jerusalem. The book of Psalms is filled with laments. Let us lament over those who suffer in war, lament over the arrogance and hardheartedness, our own hardheartedness first of all, that led to war. We follow Jesus' lead in prayer for those who would be our enemies, and with him we seek the welfare of a people diminished by decades of conflict. A Navy chaplain was shown on CNN this past week leading worship for a platoon of marines. He told them, "Pray not only for yourself but for your enemies as well. After all they are just soldiers like you, doing what they are ordered to do."[3]

Above all, O Lord, keep your servants from presumptuous sins. Keep us in Jesus.

---

3   Uwe. E. Reinhardt, "Innocents in Uniform," *New York Times*, 3/22/03, A11.

What Then Shall We Say to This?
Funeral for Matthew Heim

September 6, 2001
Romans 8:31-39
Bruce K. Modahl, Preacher

What then are we to say about these things? If God is for us, who is against us? He who did not withhold his own Son, but gave him up for all of us, will he not with him also give us everything else? Who will bring any charge against God's elect? It is God who justifies. Who is to condemn? It is Christ Jesus, who died, yes, who was raised, who is at the right hand of God, who indeed intercedes for us. Who will separate us from the love of Christ? Will hardship, or distress, or persecution, or famine, or nakedness, or peril, or sword? As it is written,

> "For your sake we are being killed all day long;
> we are accounted as sheep to be slaughtered."

No, in all these things we are more than conquerors through him who loved us. For I am convinced that neither death, nor life, nor angels, nor rulers, nor things present, nor things to come, nor powers, nor height, nor depth, nor anything else in all creation, will be able to separate us from the love of God in Christ Jesus our Lord. (Romans 8:31-39)

I preached this sermon at the funeral for a much-loved member of our congregation who committed suicide. His family gave permission for its inclusion. My prayer is that through these words, the Word of God may bring comfort to those of us who have mourned a loved one who has died in this way. I believe no one of us has escaped such grief.

You have heard the Scripture. "What then shall we say to this?" Paul asks. What then shall we say to this death, this absence, this life cut too short, this tragedy? I'll tell you one thing we shall not say. We shall not speak euphemisms. We are confident enough in God's sovereignty and grace that we can say Matt committed suicide. There it is, out in the open, exposed. But there is much more to say. How his life ended is not the sum of Matthew's life. If we shall not say euphemisms to this, what then shall we say?

Shall we say a eulogy, a good word about the one who has died? Yes. And so we have done, admirably well done in the remembrances by Matthew's friends, his godfather, and his brother. And you friends and family of Matt's will continue to remember and speak good and kind words about him. But it is not enough on its own, is it? What is eulogy to this absence and ashes and tragedy? For that is where this one life alone has ended. And the eulogy, this good word, cannot even go that far. Eulogy stops short, at least of that last hour. Eulogy is afraid of death and rightly so. Death cuts short this good word.

What then shall we say to this? There is another good word, a good word that has the power to go the distance and is not afraid of the grave. This good word goes all the way there and triumphs over death. This is God's good word, the Gospel word, the Word made flesh, the only-Son-of-God Word, Jesus Christ, who became our brother so we might become children of God. This is the Word made flesh which died as all flesh will die and then rose so that we who live in him might rise with him.

This is the Word which here must be spoken, for there is another preacher present here and present at every funeral, vying for this pulpit. This other preacher is a liar (Thomas G. Long, "Telling the Truth about Death and Life: Preaching at Funerals," *Journal for Preachers*, Easter 1997, pp. 3-12). This other preacher, of course, is death. Death is the proclaimer of evil's most convincing lie. This lying preacher tells us the grave is the end of it. God is absent. God cannot or will not keep his promises. Relationships will not last. Life is fragmented and meaningless. Death tells us God is not to be trusted. God's mercy is not wide enough and God's love not strong enough to cope with the problems we get ourselves into, Matt got himself into. Death is the only way out. Death proclaims that God's mercy is not wide enough and God's love not strong enough for Matt's death and how he died, so we have to cover it up, smooth it over with euphemisms, another kind of good word which is powerless over death. Death proclaims God is not to be trusted. And this lying preacher has a lot of evidence on his side. Dying is a powerful witness.

We have to seize the pulpit from this liar and tell the truth. And the truth is after death has spoken its loudest and ugliest, God speaks yet again. And God says, "Get up from the grave, my child." The truth is, those we love can slip from our hands but neither we nor they will ever slip out of God's hands. The truth is God has given us a gift of life that nothing can take from us. God's mercy is wider and God's love is stronger than either our despair or desperate acts. That's the truth we shall say to this.

The truth is our lives' stories are not lonely narratives, single threads spun from birth and cut off at death. Baptized into Jesus Christ, our lives' stories fit into the full and rich narrative of Christ. The threads that are our individual lives are woven by God into a tapestry of his design. We can cut the thread short. God holds us tight in his weave. We can be unfaithful by mistrusting the designer and weaver. God stays faithful to us. That's the truth we shall say to this.

By baptism Matt was adopted as God's child and given a place at the heavenly banquet table. The Spirit of God has followed Matt wherever he went. Last week Matt walked into a cul de sac named Despair. He may have felt alone, but he was not. At the moment of his despair and death, the Spirit of God ushered Matt to his seat in Jesus' presence at the heavenly banquet table. In Jesus' presence there is no more judgment. The final judgment logged against us was satisfied at the cross of Jesus Christ. In Jesus' presence faith, hope, and love abide. These three. Everything else has been cast aside.

Today, we share a foretaste, an appetizer, if you will, from the heavenly banquet. In this Holy Communion meal Jesus makes himself present to us. In his presence all judgments against us are satisfied, all guilt set aside. In his presence faith, hope, and love abide. That is the truth we have to say to this. We can trust this truth, this Jesus, with our lives today, no matter what problems we make for ourselves. We trust that God's mercy is wide and his love strong for all eternity.

One final thing we have to say to this. Trust God with your lives right now. God has given you this life, given you gifts and abilities, called you to be his. If you are feeling like you want out of life, talk to somebody, some pastor, teacher, parent, or friend. Tell them your despair. Parents, teachers, pastors, and friends, let us resolve not to avoid these words of despair because they are hard to hear from someone close to us. Let us not ignore or brush off or laugh at or call foolish the concerns that someone brings to us. Rather let us take them seriously and treat them gently. What then we shall say to this is ourselves present with one another in Jesus' name.

Amen.

Committed to Mission
Centennial Celebration

March 17, 2002
Matthew 9:1-8
Bruce K. Modahl, Preacher

And after getting into a boat he crossed the sea and came to his own town. And just then some people were carrying a paralyzed man lying on a bed. When Jesus saw their faith, he said to the paralytic, "Take heart, son; your sins are forgiven." Then some of the scribes said to themselves, "This man is blaspheming." But Jesus, perceiving their thoughts, said, "Why do you think evil in your hearts? For which is easier, to say, 'Your sins are forgiven,' or to say, 'Stand up and walk'? But so that you may know that the Son of Man has authority on earth to forgive sins"—he then said to the paralytic—"Stand up, take your bed and go to your home." And he stood up and went to his home. When the crowds saw it, they were filled with awe, and they glorified God, who had given such authority to human beings.
(Matthew 9:1-8)

In 1902 a group of people from St. John Lutheran Church in Forest Park signed a charter to start a new congregation, Grace Lutheran Church and School. On March 17, 2002, the congregation began a year-long observance in thanks to God for the 100 years of mission and ministry of the congregation. This sermon marked the beginning of that year. The sermon that follows this one brought the year to a close.

This Gospel reading celebrates mission, but peer behind this text just a short distance and we see controversy. The scribes, the Bible experts of their day, got after Jesus for healing a paralyzed man. Well, it wasn't the healing *per se* they objected to. They didn't seem to care about the paralyzed man one way or the other. "Your doctrine is all wrong," they complained to Jesus. Jesus replied, "Which is easier to say? 'Your sins are forgiven,' or 'Rise, take up your bed and walk.' But just so you know this man [pointing to himself] has authority on earth to forgive sins." With that the man got up, picked up his bed and walked on.

Following hard on that controversy was one with the Pharisees. Jesus went to dinner in the home of Matthew whom Jesus recently had called away from his toll booth to be his disciple. Matthew had his friends over to the house. The Pharisees asked Jesus' disciples, "Why does your teacher eat with such trash? You know people by the company they keep." Jesus replied, "The healthy don't need a physician do they? The sick do. I'm making a house call. Go and learn what this means, 'I desire mercy not sacrifice.' I have come to call not the righteous but sinners."

And then John the Baptist's disciples sought out Jesus, and they asked, "Why is it we lead frugal lives?" "Yes, why do you?" Jesus shot back. "Why is it we lead frugal lives," they continued, "but you and your disciples go from one big banquet to the next?" Jesus answered, "When the bridegroom is at hand the party is on."

And then Jesus got called away by a leader of the synagogue. "My little girl has just died," he tells him. Jesus goes with him, making another house call, and on the way heals a woman who has been sick for twelve years. Arriving at the house of the leader of the synagogue, Jesus tells the mourners, "She is sleeping; she is not dead." They laughed at him. They know dead when they see it. Jesus took her by the hand and raised her back into her life and family.

After Jesus goes from there, two blind men beg for their sight and then someone brought to him a man possessed by a demon. Jesus heals them, and the Pharisees conclude, "By the ruler of the demons he cast out the demons." All of this controversy Matthew crams into thirty-four verses.

Then Jesus goes on a mission trip. I need to point out this is not akin to what presidents do when the controversy gets too thick at home and they embark on a trip overseas to get away from it and generate some different headlines. No, Jesus' mission trip is into the thick of it.

He instructs his disciples, "Don't go running off to Gentile highways and Samaritan villages just yet."

This is truly remarkable. It's remarkable because controversy so quickly and easily derails mission. In fact, often times the controversy becomes the mission. Facing down scribes and Pharisees, proving them wrong, marshalling allies, outlining the debate, did not become Jesus' mission. He persisted, curing every manner of sickness, proclaiming the kingdom of God drawn near. With singleness of purpose he headed toward Jerusalem and the cross. By his death and resurrection he defeats sin, death, and devil. He opens the kingdom of heaven to all believers. That is the mission to which he is committed. It is the mission to which he commits his disciples.

Those who set out in 1902 to form Grace were likewise committed to mission. One of the most charming things I read in the minutes of Grace from 1902 was in the discussion about whom to call as the first pastor. It was duly noted, "Since we are living among Americans we must be aware there is many a soul to be saved through the English Mission work." Since we are living among Americans. Isn't that delightful. They were committed to mission. They wanted to find a pastor who knew English well enough that he could lead worship and preach in the language. The minutes say they know the pastor elected "is capable of this [and] we believe that with God's help we have found the right man." But you know this discussion must have stuck in the craw of more than one person because the minutes go on to say, "The same is true that as was said about Americans being saved through the English language, that there are many souls to be saved through the German language."

There was controversy over language and about calling a pastor. They were turned down several times before Pastor Wolter came. There was controversy with the mother congregation over debts owed and oversight of members. There was controversy over building a church building. But they were committed to mission. It was heartening to see that commitment reflected in the minutes time and again when they raised a special offering for mission work beyond their own needs.

A history of Grace published in the *Oak Leaves* back in 1924 notes that by the fifth anniversary of the congregation membership had grown by 300 percent "and so was referred to as the golden age of the congregation." Herein lies a cautionary tale for us. Controversy did derail their mission. Controversy did become their mission. The controversy was language. Despite what they said about winning souls among the Americans through the English language, they never used it. The first pastor was not successful in introducing an English service. Neither was his successor able to do this. Membership declined during those years. I have a friend who tells a story about a Swedish Lutheran Church in the 1960s in the Midwestern city where he began his ministry. The church was in a steep decline. The bishop's assistant came to meet with the leaders. He said, "The neighborhood around you is changing. The new residents speak Spanish. You still offer a service weekly in Swedish. How will they hear the Gospel in Swedish?" The congregation formed a task force to take up the challenge. A month later they asked the assistant back to look at what they were doing. As the bishop's assistant arrived, he noticed a sign out in front of the church. It read: "Everyone in the neighborhood invited. Every Saturday 10-11 a.m. Swedish Lessons." It is an apocryphal story, I'm sure.

That sign could have stood outside Grace for a good many years offering German lessons. Language was the controversy that became their mission. The Gospel mission causes controversy, always. But the controversy is not the mission, ever. Why does the mission cause controversy? What is the nature of it? Well, it is urgent. It pushes to the head of the line. I don't know about you, but I don't like people who cut in line in front of me. I mutter against them. Secondly, the Gospel mission trumps all our needs and personal likes and dislikes. The Gospel mission says those are beside the point. What is the point is doing the Gospel and getting it heard. Thirdly, the Gospel mission is an assault upon us. It dethrones the imperial "I," puts it to death, in fact. The Gospel assault, however, puts the imperial I to death in Jesus' death. With Christ we are raised a new creation and put into formation behind him in his mission.

Pastor Englebrecht was a graduate student at the University of Chicago when he accepted the call to Grace in April of 1918. He stayed four years. Under his leadership they began English services every Sunday. I am told that at one service, when he began preaching in

English many in the congregation walked out, but he kept right on. He cancelled the poorly-attended Sunday afternoon German catechism instruction and started a Sunday school in English. Some years ago Principe de Paz Iglesia Luterano, Prince of Peace Lutheran Church in Miami, started a second Sunday school, this one in English. That's commitment to mission. Pastor Englebrecht stayed four years before accepting a call to Concordia, Bronxville. Then came Pastor Geiseman, and there was no looking back. Or those who were looking back were swept along in the congregation's enthusiasm for the Gospel and commitment to its mission. That leadership and commitment to the Gospel mission continued to grow with Pastor Lueking. When controversy threatened to become the mission again in the mid-1970s, the congregation said No, we will not spend our time defending ourselves over the company we keep at this table. God is host at this table, and we are sick with sin and the brokenness of this world. We need the medicine of this food. Here God makes a house call on us. Everybody is welcome through those doors, and together we will learn what God means when God says, "I desire mercy." Jesus said, "Which is easier to say? 'Your sins are forgiven,' or 'Rise, take up your bed and walk.' But just so you know, this man has authority on earth to forgive sins." So we do, women and men, have authority on earth from our Lord Jesus Christ to forgive sins. There is no greater power.

Let us make a pact together and commit ourselves to the Gospel mission. The words of the pact are those of the creed we confess, that we are one, holy, catholic, and apostolic church. Let us banish any concern for what I like or dislike. We are not here to satisfy our personal needs. We are not here to entertain ourselves. We are called, authorized, and sent into mission. We will do whatever it takes to get the Gospel a hearing. Let us strive to find the best way to form disciples for Jesus Christ.

The bridegroom is at hand. The party is on.

Responding to the Promise
Centennial Celebration

March 16, 2003
Mark 10:35-45
Bruce K. Modahl, Preacher

James and John, the sons of Zebedee, came forward to him and said to him, "Teacher, we want you to do for us whatever we ask of you." And he said to them, "What is it you want me to do for you?" And they said to him, "Grant us to sit, one at your right hand and one at your left, in your glory." But Jesus said to them, "You do not know what you are asking. Are you able to drink the cup that I drink, or be baptized with the baptism that I am baptized with?" They replied, "We are able." Then Jesus said to them, "The cup that I drink you will drink; and with the baptism with which I am baptized, you will be baptized; but to sit at my right hand or at my left is not mine to grant, but it is for those for whom it has been prepared."

When the ten heard this, they began to be angry with James and John. So Jesus called them and said to them, "You know that among the Gentiles those whom they recognize as their rulers lord it over them, and their great ones are tyrants over them. But it is not so among you; but whoever wishes to become great among you must be your servant, and whoever wishes to be first among you must be slave of all. For the Son of Man came not to be served but to serve, and to give his life a ransom for many." (Mark 10:35-45)

In this sermon I mention the Church Vocations Initiative and First Call. The former began when we realized that it had been fifteen years since a member of Grace began a church vocation. Since the inception of the Church Vocations Initiative, Grace has supported many in their college and seminary education who are now serving the church in parish ministry, as teachers, and in other callings. First Call was an attempt to continue the calling God gave us at our baptism.

Yearly, a theologian of the church came to preach and teach among us to further ground us in our calling. First Call continued for about five years. Though First Call no longer exists, the endeavor continues. We see that in the adult education opportunities every Sunday, in new member classes, Sunday school, Confirmation, and in a robust youth and family ministry.

The history of our congregation is the story of how those who have gone before us responded to the promise of grace. That is how Martin Marty frames our history. I had a chance to read Marty's book about our congregation before it went to the printer. He concludes a chapter on a particularly difficult period in our history with the line, "There remained the congregation's always-in-process responding to the promise of Grace."

That's who we are. That's who our history shows us to be: A congregation always in the process of responding to the promise of Grace. But what is the promise? How we define the promise will make a great difference in how we respond and therefore a great difference in our future.

James and John in the Gospel reading are responding to a promise. It is easy to be hard on James and John, these sons of Zebedee, who come looking to Jesus for special favors. But I'm thinking maybe they simply are looking for reassurance about the future. Oh, sure, they could have asked for something less than being prime minister and secretary of state when Jesus comes into his inheritance. But there is no harm in asking, is there?

They are looking to Jesus for some reassurance about the future. That is no less than any one of us is looking for from him. It is what we as a congregation are looking for at the end of this centennial year and peer with some trepidation up the road. The theme we are considering for this next year is drawn from Psalm 90, as was the theme for this centennial year. This year's you see on the banner, the first verse of Psalm 90: "Lord you have been our dwelling place in all generations." For next year we are considering the last verse, "Lord, prosper the work of our hands." It sounds more polite than what James and John asked, but I'm not sure it is much different in substance. Lord, you do promise us a good future, right, a flourishing ministry, a community growing in love and good deeds. And just think of all the good that James and John would do as Jesus' left and right hand men when he comes in glory.

They are asking for some clarity about what Jesus promises for the future. They have heard talk of suffering and at the transfiguration had a vision of the resurrection. And it hasn't been easy so far. Jesus is leading. James and John and the rest are following his lead. He has rushed them from one town's tent revival meeting and immediately on to the next, from one village's sick and demon-possessed and immediately on to another. So far he has led them into conflict with the scribes and the Pharisees, the people who are in charge of much in life and can make life miserable for a person. He takes the turn in the road uphill towards Jerusalem, and they were not singing Psalm 122 as our choir sang today. They were not glad when Jesus said to them, "Let us go to the house of the Lord that our feet may be within your gates, O Jerusalem." Their psalm ran more along the lines of, "What is he getting us into? Have we reached the point of no return?" Jesus is up ahead, walking fast. They are still back at the crossroad, dragging their feet, complaining of blisters. So, Jesus spells out for the third time what lies ahead, only this time in more detail. I'm not sure why he thought it would allay their fears for him to say, "See, we are going up to Jerusalem, and I will be handed over to the chief priests and the scribes, and they will condemn me to death; then they will hand me over to the Gentiles; they will mock me and spit on me and flog me and kill me and after three days I will rise again."

It is right after this that James and John come asking their favor. They are responding to the promise of resurrection, but they have not understood the promise. They try to secure their place at Jesus' victory banquet, but they don't understand what it means to drink the cup from that table. They hope to be called "Your Excellency." They will fight it out later about which gets to be prime minister and which secretary of state, and don't think these brothers would not fight about who gets to be boss of whom.

Jesus says, "You are writing yourselves into the wrong story and headed up the wrong road. This is Gentile power, the power that mocks, spits, flogs, and finally kills. You don't understand the promise. You are responding to the old order's promise of the gain to be had by lording it over others." Think corporate ladder, climbing to the top. We should not be so quick to trash this model. The higher you climb means the better you are at what you do, the fewer peers you have, the more excellence you have achieved. It also means having more people under you. And often some of those get stepped on in the climb up. And once you get into that rarefied air, then what? Think tower of Babel, climbing up to God, to storm heaven. Think Grace tower. That may sound like heresy on our celebration day. But that's what the charge was when the church was built: "A tower of Babel in River Forest, building this extravagance in the midst of The Great Depression, a sign of their pride. They think they are superior." There was as much jealousy in 1930 as the ten showed James and John in AD 30. This is what Gentile power produces, and worse. It has no future.

Jesus says, "I came not to be served but to serve and to give my life as a ransom." Here is the promise. He is Lord, alright. But he doesn't lord it over us. He lords it under us. He underlords us all the way to the grave in order to ransom us from death. He turns Gentile power on its head. At the pinnacle is his cross, bearing the weight of the world.

Jesus further promised James and John, "You will be able to drink the cup I will drink. You will be baptized with my baptism." Right now James and John don't have a clue what that means. They have been looking for it to be easy. And it is not going to be easy. "It is going to get harder, James and John, but you will be able." That's the promise.

James and John responded to the promise. They followed in fits and starts. There wasn't anything easy or perfect about it. We respond to the promise. Grace tower is a symbol of that response. Built on the foundation that is Christ, its height is not the height to which we aspire but the amount of ministry God calls us to bear. We are a people always in process of responding to the promise of Grace. That's who our history shows us to be. The character of this congregation was revealed in what was perhaps the most difficult period in our history, the decision to leave the Lutheran Church–Missouri Synod and the lengthy litigation that followed as they tried to take this property. As Marty tells the story in his book, there were some in the congregation who mourned leaving Missouri. Probably still are. There were others who rejoiced over it. Probably still are. Marty applies the "as though" dialectic that Paul uses in 1 Corinthians to explain the character of this congregation. Paul says, "Let those who mourn be as though they were not mourning, and those who rejoice as though they were not rejoicing." Marty writes, "So at Grace, those who mourned the division had to live 'as though' they had no reason to mourn; those who rejoiced in the changes were to live 'as though' they had no reason to rejoice." The purpose of this "as though" living was so they might focus "on the good news of what God was doing in Jesus Christ among them" and get on with that ministry. Their response to the promise was to be subject to one another out of reverence for Christ.

Our always-in-process response to the promise is evident more recently. With our offerings lagging behind last year we struggled to pay those called to serve here and we sent very little of our promised support to the many struggling ministries that depend on us to one degree or another. I told you at the end of January that this is not who we are and you said, "That's true." And we responded to the promise and are now close and will certainly make the goal of having our support up to date by Easter.

What of the future? Legacy of Grace is a response to the promise. It is our thank offering for where we have been and our investment in the future. It is what will enable our creative responses to the promise, such as our Church Vocation Initiative and First Call. There is a crisis of leadership in the church. We have responded to the promise by beginning to identify, encourage, and support those with gifts for ministry to be pastors, teachers, musicians, and directors of Christian education. First Call is a response to the promise by providing for the formation of leaders and church members who will know what the promise is and lead in our response to it.

None of this will be easy. But Jesus says to us, "You will be able." We take the cup from Jesus' victory banquet. We will never understand completely all that it means to drink the cup from that table until "we on that final journey go that Christ is for us preparing; we'll gather in song, our hearts aglow, all joy of the heavens sharing, and walk in the light of God's own grace, with angels his name adoring" (LBW hymn 161, "O Day Full of Grace).

Do you long to sing this song with full organ and brass accompaniment? May that longing, that anticipation drive your response to the promise.

Conspiracy Theory
The Retirement of Pastor Phyllis Kersten

April 19, 2008
John 20:19-23
Bruce K. Modahl, Preacher

> When it was evening on that day, the first day of the week, and the doors of the house where the disciples had met were locked for fear of the Jews, Jesus came and stood among them and said, "Peace be with you." After he said this, he showed them his hands and his side. Then the disciples rejoiced when they saw the Lord. Jesus said to them again, "Peace be with you. As the Father has sent me, so I send you." When he had said this, he breathed on them and said to them, "Receive the Holy Spirit. If you forgive the sins of any, they are forgiven them; if you retain the sins of any, they are retained." (John 20:19-23)

This sermon is brief. Its brevity is not because I did not have much to say about Pastor Kersten but because so many others had things they wanted to say. I mention in the sermon that with her retirement she begins a whole new chapter in her ministry. That new chapter included interim ministries, supply preaching, and in 2015 it brought her back to Grace as interim associate pastor. She is a gentle, patient, loving, and loyal servant of God, and my friend.

I begin the way Paul (with one exception) always began his letters. "I give thanks to God always for you. Phyllis, in my heart, in my prayers, and in the day-in and day-out routines of working together I give thanks to God for you.

A few Sundays ago the gospel reading was the story of Doubting Thomas. You preached on that text and as I remember you did your best to rehabilitate Thomas. That is just like you Phyllis, looking for the best in everyone, holding out hope against hope for reclamation and reconciliation. In that text are these verses,

> When it was evening on that day, the first day of the week, and the doors of the house where the disciples had met were locked. . . . Jesus came and stood among them and said, "Peace be with you." After he said this, he showed them his hands and his side. Then the disciples rejoiced when they saw the Lord. Jesus said to them again, "Peace be with you. As the Father has sent me, so I send you." When he had said this, he breathed on them and said to them, "Receive the Holy Spirit. If you forgive the sins of any, they are forgiven them; if you retain the sins of any, they are retained."

The part I am interested in is the infusion of Jesus' breath into their lives. Infusion is the Greek word, *enephusesen*, to be exact. The infusion of Jesus' breath bore the Holy Spirit into the lives of Jesus' disciples. Jesus' breath was the source of their inspiration. Spirit is at the heart of the word inspiration. We hear spirit in there, the spirit in us, inspiring us. The Holy Spirit is at the heart of Phyllis's ministry among us. Jesus' breath, breathing in her is her inspiration.

There are other words that have spirit at their heart, words related to inspire and inspiration, words that reveal also the heart of Pastor Kersten's ministry. Respiration is one of them. We depend on a reliable respiration for our lives. There is no life without breath going in and out. Respiration is descriptive also of the Holy Spirit's movement, propelling our lives forward as God's spirit people. The Spirit breathes us out onto the world.

Perspire is another of these words. The prefix *per* means "through." Not sweat, but the spirit comes through Phyllis in her ministry. And then there is the word expire, though we probably shouldn't bring that up at a retirement event. Phyllis has not reached her expiration date by any means. The Spirit will breathe through her in a whole new chapter of her life and ministry.

Conspire is the word I'm aiming for. Conspiracy has a sinister sound to it but it simply means "to breathe with." And in our usage it would be the Holy Spirit breathing with us. It has been my privilege to be Phyllis's co-conspirator in ministry these ten years. The Holy Spirit has drawn us together in the conspiracy of making Christ known and offering Christ's comfort.

Paul ended his letters by sending his greetings to various people he knew or knew of in the churches to which he wrote. With this sort of closing Paul indicates a continuance to their relationship and their ministry. So, in closing, Phyllis I send you, my co-conspirator in the Gospel, my warmest greetings.

One Little Word

God's Mighty Music Service

July 27, 2014
1 Samuel 17
Bruce K. Modahl, Preacher

Now David was the son of an Ephrathite of Bethlehem in Judah, named Jesse, who had eight sons. . . . David said to the men who stood by him, "What shall be done for the man who kills this Philistine, and takes away the reproach from Israel? For who is this uncircumcised Philistine that he should defy the armies of the living God?" . . .

Then he took his staff in his hand, and chose five smooth stones from the wadi, and put them in his shepherd's bag, in the pouch; his sling was in his hand, and he drew near to the Philistine. . . .

When the Philistine looked and saw David, he disdained him, for he was only a youth, ruddy and handsome in appearance. The Philistine said to David, "Am I a dog, that you come to me with sticks?" And the Philistine cursed David by his gods. The Philistine said to David, "Come to me, and I will give your flesh to the birds of the air and to the wild animals of the field." But David said to the Philistine, "You come to me with sword and spear and javelin; but I come to you in the name of the Lord of hosts, the God of the armies of Israel, whom you have defied. This very day the Lord will deliver you into my hand, and I will strike you down and cut off your head; and I will give the dead bodies of the Philistine army this very day to the birds of the air and to the wild animals of the earth, so that all the earth may know that there is a God in Israel, and that all this assembly may know that the Lord does not save by sword and spear; for the battle is the Lord's and he will give you into our hand." (1 Samuel 17:12, 26, 38-40, 42-47)

On the afternoon of July 27, 2014, Grace brought a full orchestra and choir to lead worship under a canopy pitched in a vacant lot adjoining Harmony Community Church. The setting was on a busy road with a noisy "L" line running right across the street. The choir sang in German the cantata Bach composed based on the hymn, "A Mighty Fortress." They were joined by the gospel team, praise band, and a spoken word artist from Harmony. We called the service "God's Mighty Music." The pastor of Harmony is James Brooks. He served as youth minister at Grace until becoming the senior pastor at Harmony following his father's retirement. Harmony is located in the North Lawndale neighborhood of Chicago. The neighborhood is challenged by poverty, crime, and gun violence. The neighborhood is not defined by these things but rather by the promises of God embodied in the hope and actions of churches such as Harmony. The congregation that afternoon came from Grace, Harmony, and the neighborhood. I had the privilege of preaching for the service. Pastor Michael Costello, the cantor at Grace masterminded the logistics for this event. In the words of one of our co-workers, "Pastor Costello makes things happen." He would add, "To the Glory of God."

Martin Luther said, "The devil, the originator of sorrowful anxieties and restless troubles, flees before the sound of music almost as much as before the Word of God."

I'd say if the Word of God is combined with the music, the devil flees double time. And who would have imagined what we have done here today. We have the gospel team, and praise band, and a spoken word artist from Harmony Community Church. And we have a cantata composed by Johann Sebastian Bach from the choir and musicians of Grace Lutheran Church and School. With that combination I say the devil has left the premises, at least for now. It will always be prowling around. That's why we have to keep singing. We know that by Jesus' death on the cross and resurrection from the dead he defeated sin, death, and the devil. God will bring that victory to completion on the day of Jesus' return. The devil is mortally wounded. But, like any mortally wounded animal, the devil remains dangerous. So, we have to keep singing, and praying, and marching, and working at making peace in order to stem the violence.

Some may ask, "Why do you care? You come from a comfortable suburb far removed from our problems." John Donne is a writer from centuries ago. He said, "The church is universal, so are all her actions; all that she does belongs to all. When she baptizes someone, that action concerns me; for that person is thereby connected to the body of Christ of which I am a part because of my baptism. We baptized people of God are part of the same body with Jesus Christ as our head. And when the church buries a person, that action concerns me: all humankind is of one author. . . . Any person's death diminishes me, because I am involved in humankind." That ancient writer eloquently expresses why it is we care.

The cantata is based on a hymn written by Martin Luther. The hymn is "A Mighty Fortress Is Our God." One of the verses says,

> Though hordes of devils fill the land
> All threat'ning to devour us,
> We tremble not, unmoved we stand;
> They cannot overpow'r us.
> Let this world's tyrant rage;
> In battle we'll engage!
> His might is doomed to fail;
> God's judgment must prevail!
> One little word subdues him.

When I hear Pastor Brooks preach I often hear him say, "Can I get a witness?" At first I thought he was asking for someone in the congregation to witness to their faith or give him some support, an "Amen" or a "Preach on." But I soon discovered he meant a witness from Scripture. So, can I get a witness? In the book of 1 Samuel we learn the Philistines were the thugs threatening the neighborhoods, towns, and cities in which the people of Israel lived. They intimidated the people of Israel. The people in the neighborhoods, towns, and cities of Israel were afraid. The Philistines had the best weapons, weapons of iron. The Israelites only had bronze weapons that could not stand up to iron. The Philistines raided, stole, and killed. They didn't care who they killed—men, women, and children. It seemed no one could stop them. Finally it came to a showdown. The Philistines gathered their armies for battle. King Saul gathered the armies of Israel and formed ranks against the Philistines. The Philistines stood on a mountain on one side, and the Israelites stood on a mountain on the other side with a valley between them. The Philistines had a champion named Goliath. You know about Goliath. He was ten feet tall. His armor weighed 150 lbs. His spear weighed 19 lbs. The only thing I could do with a 19 lb. spear is drop it. Every day he came down into the valley and called up to the armies of Israel, "Someone come and fight me. If I win the people of Israel do whatever we say. If you win, we'll do whatever you want. What's the matter, are you chicken? Is there no one who will come and fight me?" This went on for forty days. No one would come and fight Goliath.

David's three older brothers were in the army. David was too young. But he came every once in a while with food for his brothers. He heard Goliath's taunts. He said, "Who is this fool who defies the armies of the living God. I'll go and fight him." His oldest brother was angry with him for talking like this. But King Saul heard about it and thought, "This is the first volunteer we've had. Why not?" So he put his own armor on David. But David was so small he could not move. He took the armor off. He went down to the creek bed. He picked out five small, smooth stones and put them in his pouch. Then he went out to meet Goliath. Goliath laughed. He said, "I'm going to cut you in pieces and feed you to the pigeons." David said, "You come to me with sword and spear and javelin, but I come to you in the name of the Lord of hosts." David ran at him. As he ran he pulled one of those small, smooth stones from his pouch and placed it in his sling, the same sling he used to fend off bears and lions from his father's flocks of sheep. He swung the sling overhead. He flung the stone from the sling. It struck Goliath in the forehead, and down he went. The Philistines fled that day. Israel was free of their violence.

One small stone felled Goliath. One little word subdues the raging tyrant, the devil. We need to be careful here. Those who do the violence are not devils. They are our sons and daughters, our brothers and sisters. Many of them were baptized in the same water that carried us to Jesus. But the Evil One uses fear, anger, jealousy, greed, drugs, and a host of other things on people to create mayhem in our communities.

We know the little word, Jesus, and the promises that come with his resurrection from the dead. Our calling is to speak and sing that word to our own fear and to those who would make us afraid. Jesus promises to reclaim all our lives to serve as a part of his redeemed and new creation.

There are signs of that new creation all around us—the churches in our communities, the food pantries, ministries like Lawndale Christian Health Center, and the daily neighborliness that we show one another.

We cannot remain silent. With violence all around us we must sing the name that is above all names.

> The name of Jesus charms our fears
> And bids our sorrows cease,
> Sings music in the sinner's ears,
> Brings life and health and peace.
>
> He breaks the pow'r of canceled sin;
> He sets the pris'ner free.
> His blood can make the foulest clean;
> His blood avails for me.
>
> To God all glory, praise and love
> Be now and ever giv'n
> By saints below and saints above,
> The Church in earth and heav'n.

A Step Too Far
The Twelfth Sunday after Pentecost

August 31, 2014
Matthew 16:21-28
Bruce K. Modahl, Preacher

From that time on, Jesus began to show his disciples that he must go to Jerusalem and undergo great suffering at the hands of the elders and chief priests and scribes, and be killed, and on the third day be raised. And Peter took him aside and began to rebuke him, saying, "God forbid it, Lord! This must never happen to you." But he turned and said to Peter, "Get behind me, Satan! You are a stumbling block to me; for you are setting your mind not on divine things but on human things."

Then Jesus told his disciples, "If any want to become my followers, let them deny themselves and take up their cross and follow me. For those who want to save their life will lose it, and those who lose their life for my sake will find it. For what will it profit them if they gain the whole world but forfeit their life? Or what will they give in return for their life?

"For the Son of Man is to come with his angels in the glory of his Father, and then he will repay everyone for what has been done. Truly I tell you, there are some standing here who will not taste death before they see the Son of Man coming in his kingdom." (Matthew 16:21-28)

I preached this sermon on the Sunday of my retirement. I began my ministry at Grace on September 1, 1998, and completed it sixteen years to the day. It was a wonderful sixteen years of shared ministry with the people of God at Grace.

"You have carried this too far," is an admonition we have heard and an admonition we have spoken. What the "this" is varies according to circumstances. However, there is a constant in all the variety.

An employee on a construction project involving heights similar to the height of our tower consistently cut corners on the safety rules. When the foreman caught him on top of a tall structure and then another six feet in the air standing on a foot square pedestal without a safety harness, he told the employee, "Get down from there and get your safety belt now." The employee started to argue with him. The foreman said, "You have carried this too far."

It seems to me carrying something a step too far means stepping out ahead of the one you should be following or at least working with. More than that, carrying whatever this is too far implies we've come to the breaking point. You're going to get your pink slip, be sent to your room, forced into rehab, spend the night on the couch, and so forth.

Both Jeremiah and Peter heard a version of this admonition from God. Jeremiah regularly complained to God about the difficulty of his assignment. And it was difficult. His friends turned against him. Family members plotted to assassinate him because he brought shame on the family. Only one other prophet took his side. That would be like all the pastors in the country except one opposed him. One of the royal family had soldiers throw him into a pit. He got death threats all the time. Marriage, family, and a normal life were out of the question for him.

God listened to Jeremiah's complaints with varying degrees of patience, answered with words of encouragement, and promised more than an invisible presence. God promised to act on Jeremiah's behalf.

In his first proclamation to the people Jeremiah called God "the fountain of living waters, not like the cracked cisterns that can hold no water, which are the foreign gods you worship." In today's first reading, Jeremiah concludes his complaint saying, "Truly, you God are to me like a deceitful brook, like waters that fail." This is when God responds, "You have carried this a step too far. With these words you have stepped out ahead of me. All I see is your back. I cancel my call to you. You are no longer my prophet. You are on your own. We are through."

But instead of stepping away, God took a step toward Jeremiah saying, "If you turn back, I will take you back, and you shall stand before me. If you utter what is precious and not what is worthless, you shall serve as my mouth." God recalled Jeremiah to service. Jeremiah did turn back to God. He continued his ministry and lived to complain another day.

Luther called the church a "mouth house." It is where we give voice to the Gospel. Luther further said when the Gospel is proclaimed Jesus himself walks among us. In my ministry with you I have sought to be God's mouth. I begin sermon preparation with the prayer, "God give me the words." Somewhere in the course of the week I ask God to gather a congregation and prepare them to hear. As I step into the pulpit I pray, "Dear God, preach your word through me." Where I have failed I depend on your forbearance. Mostly I depend on God's grace. I have never found writing a sermon to be easy. I regularly complain to God about it. When I have carried my complaint a step too far, I always discover God taking a step toward me and saying, "Quit your whining, tie your shoes, get up off the floor, and let's get on with it. Don't be afraid. I am with you." I expect to hear the same word from God in this next phase of life.

In last week's Gospel reading Jesus heaped praise on Simon for identifying Jesus as the Messiah. He renamed him *Petros*, rock. He said "On this rock I will build my church, and the gates of hell will not prevail against it." In today's reading Jesus explained to the disciples and explains to us what it means that he is the Messiah. It is not an easy lesson. He will have to go over this again and again. It means he must suffer, be killed, and on the third day be raised. That is not what the disciples expected of Messiah. Suffering was not in their dictionary entry for Messiah. They expected Messiah to be a king like David only supercharged. Jesus words so shook them I doubt they even heard anything about being raised from the dead. Or maybe they did but that sounded even more preposterous than a suffering Messiah.

Peter took him aside to get him back on message. Sometimes Peter acts more like petrified than *petros*. He acts like a campaign manager whose candidate has wandered off script. Jesus turned and said in effect, "You have taken this a step too far. You are on the wrong side from me. You are taking sides with Satan when the Evil One tempted me to avoid the cross." Peter the rock crumbled into a stumbling block for his Lord. In his commentary Tom Long says, "Jesus saw Peter's efforts not to 'take him aside' but to pull him off course." Stanley Hauerwas wrote, "Peter has joined the ranks of those who want Jesus to accept the world as it is."

Seeking to serve as God's mouth, I have sought to proclaim the cross. Every week the question I bring to the text is, "Why do I need a crucified and risen Savior?" For Lutherans the purpose of preaching is to necessitate the cross in our lives. It's an awkward phrase but it's the one that comes closest to the awkwardness of the task. The German phrase is *Was treibt Christum*, literally "what pushes Christ." We preachers are Christ pushers.

The confirmands take notes on the worship service. In the form they use there are a couple of questions about the sermon. One of the questions is "What did you hear about God?" In response to one of my sermons a confirmand wrote, "Nothing, really." Where that has been the case, I depend again on your forbearance. And mostly I depend on hearing from Jesus what he said to Peter, "Get behind me." Behind Jesus is where a disciple belongs. Jesus does not step away from Peter. He steps toward him. Peter assumes the place of a disciple, following Jesus, and trying again.

Some chapters ago in Matthew's Gospel Jesus told the disciples, "Whoever does not take up the cross and follow me is not worthy of me." Now he tells them this cross talk is not a metaphor at all. At the cross God steps toward us. God in Christ shoulders our sin, suffers the same horrific violence we, who are created in God's image, unleash on one another in the streets of Chicago and Ferguson, Missouri, in Nigeria, Gaza, Israel, Iraq, Syria, and the list goes on. He died as we must die. On the third day he did rise from the grave. He ascended into heaven. We follow him on that path to resurrection and new life. This new life is now and forever. We join Jesus as those who refuse to accept the world as it is. We know the day is coming when blood will no longer run in the streets and the Prince of Peace will reign. He does not leave us with vague promises about his invisible presence. He is present in ways that we hear and touch and taste. He is present in the Word. Jesus is present in the waters of baptism. There we are joined to his death and resurrection. By baptism the Holy Spirit takes up residence in us. If we ever doubt God's presence in our lives, we have only to trace our hands through that water and perhaps use that wet hand to trace the sign of the cross on our bodies. Jesus is truly flesh and blood present to us in the bread and wine of the Lord's Supper. And he is present in what Luther called the mutual conversation and consolation of the people of God.

Jesus tells us to take up our cross and follow. Today hundreds of thousands of people are doing just that. Thousands of Christians have been and continue to be executed in Iraq by the forces of ISIS because they refuse to renounce their faith. Over 200,000 Christians fled the city of Mosul in Iraq when ISIS swept in. They took refuge in Nineveh, and are now once again on the run. For some reason we have not heard much about them. We bear the cross when we care, learn as much as we can about the suffering of others, pray for them, contribute to their relief, and lift up our voices on their behalf. The church of Christ does not play defense. Jesus said the gates of hell will not prevail against us. That means we are on the offense against the forces that want us to acquiesce to the world as it is. We know that a new day is coming. That new day is at hand in Jesus and in Jesus' people.

www.ingramcontent.com/pod-product-compliance
Lightning Source LLC
Chambersburg PA
CBHW072023110526
44592CB00012B/1411